BREAKING THE HUDDLE

How Your Community Can Grow Its Witness

**DON EVERTS,
DOUG SCHAUPP,
AND VAL GORDON**

D0167819

IVP Books

An imprint of InterVarsity Press
Downers Grove, Illinois

InterVarsity Press
P.O. Box 1400, Downers Grove, IL 60515-1426
ivpress.com
email@ivpress.com

©2016 by Donald D. Everts II, Douglas R. Schaupp, and Valerie Gordon

InterVarsity Press® is the book-publishing division of InterVarsity Christian Fellowship/USA®, a movement of students and faculty active on campus at hundreds of universities, colleges and schools of nursing in the United States of America, and a member movement of the International Fellowship of Evangelical Students. For information about local and regional activities, visit intervarsity.org.

All Scripture quotations, unless otherwise indicated, are taken from THE HOLY BIBLE, NEW INTERNATIONAL VERSION®, NIV® Copyright © 1973, 1978, 1984, 2011 by Biblica, Inc.™ Used by permission. All rights reserved worldwide.

While any stories in this book are true, some names and identifying information may have been changed to protect the privacy of individuals.

Figures 4.2, 5.2, and 6.2 are used by permission of InterVarsity Christian Fellowship.

Cover design: Cindy Kiple
Interior design: Beth McGill
Images: © GoodWeen123/iStockphoto

ISBN 978-0-8308-4491-3 (print)
ISBN 978-0-8308-8306-6 (digital)

Printed in the United States of America ∞

Library of Congress Cataloging-in-Publication Data
A catalog record for this book is available from the Library of Congress.

P	20	19	18	17	16	15	14	13	12	11	10	9	8	7	6	5	4	3	2	1
Y	33	32	31	30	29	28	27	26	25	24	23	22	21	20	19	18	17	16

We dedicate this book to all our children:

Simon Francis Everts

Teya Terese Everts

Victor Wayne Everts

Mark Lee Schaupp

David Lee Schaupp

Stephanie Haejin Schaupp

Sadie Elizabeth Gordon

Tate Alexander Gordon

Kai David Gordon

This book is for your generation.
May God help his church flourish so that as
you step into leadership in the coming years, you
will get to be a part of great God movements and
conversion communities. May God grow
your faith so that you can lead in faith.

Now having been questioned by the Pharisees as to when the kingdom of God was coming, [Jesus] answered them and said, "The kingdom of God is not coming with signs to be observed; nor will they say, 'Look, here it is!' or, 'There it is!' For behold, the kingdom of God is in your midst."

LUKE 17:20-21 NASB

CONTENTS

INTRODUCTION

A Case for Hope

Since the early 1990s there has been an ongoing conversation about what Christian witness looks like (or needs to look like) in our new, postmodern context. This conversation has led some people to a cynical place (*Postmodern folks just don't seem all that interested in Christianity!*) and others to a genuinely confused place (*Evangelism as I know it just doesn't seem to be working anymore!*). It has led the three of us to a genuinely hopeful place. And that's why we've written this book.

Our own foray into this wonderful conversation about witness in a postmodern context began as we encountered and interacted with a set of findings called the five thresholds of postmodern conversion.

THE STORY OF THE FIVE THRESHOLDS

Let's go back to the early 1990s. I (Doug) loved using C. S. Lewis's *Mere Christianity* to engage with seekers and help them decide to follow Jesus.[1] This approach worked for me in college (sort of), so I assumed it should keep working. Except it stopped working. So I began experimenting. I tried all manner of crazy and creative ways of doing evangelism that might possibly connect with my local context of 1990s Los Angeles. Most of these harebrained ideas bore very little fruit.

But in 1996 things hit a boiling point. I was helping lead an evangelistic small group filled with seekers. Even though the non-Christians stayed involved for a whopping thirty weeks, no one became a follower of Jesus. Not one. I was at a complete loss, and frankly I was fed up. I had no language or tools to understand what was going on with the non-Christians and what I could have done differently. I was passionate about being more "seeker-sensitive" in order to help lead more people toward Jesus, but my somewhat simplistic lens on evangelism and conversion didn't give me any insight on how to proceed.

This seemingly fruitless small group, along with a number of other experiences at the time, led to a significant amount of godly discontentment in my life and in my leadership. Because I like to collaborate and learn alongside others, I gathered a group of fellow leaders for a day-long retreat together and jumped into this important topic. These leaders from the trenches asked, "What if the journey toward Jesus were more complex than we previously thought? What phases do non-Christians seem to go through?" We then shared stories from our own local contexts of people journeying toward Jesus—some who had journeyed all the way and others whose journeys had seemed to peter out—to see what we could learn and try to discern any patterns.

By taking seriously the stories of these non-Christians and new Christians, my colleagues and I began to discern striking similarities. Not only were there similar thresholds that non-Christians passed through on their journeys, but (surprisingly) many passed through them in pretty much the same order. My friends and I summarized these similarities in what we called "the five thresholds of postmodern conversion." And then we set about testing our tentative findings.

On college campuses throughout Southern California we tested the five thresholds, listening to more stories of new Christians, to see if there really was something to this basic contour of the path to Jesus in a postmodern context. We invited other partners in the gospel to look at the five thresholds in light of conversions they were seeing in their local contexts—to mess with the five thresholds, take away a threshold, add a threshold. We weren't interested in the five thresholds per se, but we were interested in better understanding how people were becoming Christians in our postmodern context. Surprisingly, five years later the five thresholds were still standing!

We began to realize that all these new Christians (over two thousand of them) and non-Christians we were talking with had given us a real gift with their honest stories: they had described, it seemed, something real and solid about how people journey to faith these days. Additionally, we were beginning to experience significant fruit from putting the insights of the five thresholds to use. Better understanding our non-Christian friends helped us empathize and better serve our friends right where they were in their journeys. It seemed that more people were becoming Christians. At that point my colleagues and I began actively "giving away" the five thresholds: putting this wisdom tool about postmodern conversion out there to see what others might do with it, how it might be helpful to others, if it really had legs.

This was about the time that I (Val) encountered the five thresholds. I was working with college students and staff with Inter-Varsity Christian Fellowship in New England who were intentionally asking this question: How do we meet students on campus who might never set foot in an InterVarsity meeting? I have always been committed to evangelism but am in no way a natural evangelist. When I first bumped into the five thresholds in 1999, it gave me a basic framework to carry around with me. I found myself referencing the five thresholds in my head as I talked with non-Christians. I had a better sense of what kind of conversation the person I was talking with might be ready for. While my mind had always been filled with an endless list of things I could potentially talk about, the five thresholds helped me discern which of those things might actually be helpful. I could almost feel and hear the thresholds during my conversations. Learning which threshold someone might be at began to shape which part of my own story I would share and which Scripture story might have the most impact.

I also found the five thresholds helping me mentor younger Christians as well, and over time I started using my God-given leadership gifts to equip and train others with the five thresholds wherever I went. My consulting and training work, informed by the five thresholds, began to lead to more natural and fruitful witness for hundreds of people and dozens of Christian communities across the country. Through this process I have become a shameless fan of this wisdom tool that non-Christians and new Christians have given the church through their honest stories.

The same is true for me (Don). Introverted by temperament, I have always struggled with witness. I grudgingly participated in a few "contact evangelism" experiences in college in Tacoma, Washington, but felt very awkward and over time had become somewhat allergic to witness. Even when I became a Christian leader and missionary on campus with InterVarsity, sharing my faith with others and engaging with non-Christians always remained on the back burner for me. To be honest, I preferred to interact with Christians.

This began to change in 1997 when I moved to Boulder, Colorado, and found myself surrounded by fascinating, engaging, nonchurched "normal people" who knew nothing about Christianity and Jesus. Interacting with non-Christians and helping them learn about Jesus was no longer avoidable, and I began to ask this question: How do you introduce people to Jesus in ways that aren't cheesy or cliché or rude? Wrestling with this question not only led me to write my first book, *Jesus with Dirty Feet*,[2] but also fueled a curiosity to learn from other leaders how to engage in natural, helpful witness.

So when I encountered the five thresholds, I began applying them personally in my relationships with non-Christians and introducing them to my fellow campus missionaries and students in Colorado. I not only found my own witness growing more free and natural and fruitful but saw the effect this portable framework had in growing the empathy, compassion, and witness of the staff and students I worked with.

By the time Doug and I had a chance conversation in 2005, the five thresholds had made their way into ministries throughout the

United States and several other countries by word of mouth. The five thresholds seemed to be genuinely helpful as people asked two important questions:

- How do people come to Jesus in our postmodern context?
- How can Christians best help their friends on that journey?

To help fuel that ongoing conversation around those two questions Doug and I gathered stories, insights, practical applications, and findings that had grown up around the five thresholds over the last decade and published them in *I Once Was Lost: What Postmodern Skeptics Taught Us About Their Path to Jesus.*[3] This introduced the church and Christians in the United States and beyond to the five thresholds of postmodern conversion.

A SUMMARY OF THE FIVE THRESHOLDS

I Once Was Lost remains the most comprehensive description of the five thresholds and the most in-depth exploration of how Christians can apply these insights to better understand and serve their non-Christian friends. Video training on the five thresholds is also available through InterVarsity Christian Fellowship.[4] However, the five thresholds are simple enough to be remembered with five basic pictures, shown in figure I.1.

| TRUST | CURIOSITY | CHANGE | SEEKING | FOLLOWER |

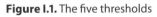

Figure I.1. The five thresholds

Based on our friends' stories about their own journeys to Jesus, it seems that quite often skeptics must face five relatively distinct thresholds as they make their way to faith in Jesus.

Threshold #1: From distrust to trust. Because of the amount of distrust that exists toward Christianity, the church, and Christians, it is paramount that trust be established between a non-Christian and at least one Christian. Most of our friends' conversion stories begin something like this: "I had been hurt by the church and didn't want to have anything to do with Christians. But then I met this guy at work . . ." And then they tell the often unremarkable story of developing trust with an actual Christian. Given the amount of church-hurt that exists in the world, this is a crucial part of a non-Christian's journey that needs to be understood.

Threshold #2: From indifference to curiosity. Even when someone trusts a Christian for the first time, it doesn't necessarily follow that there will be an interest in that Christian's faith. Many people today are actually quite indifferent about Christianity and, even worse, about Jesus himself. Our friends have told us a variety of ways that their interest in Jesus was piqued and how that was a crucial part of their journey forward. Note that crossing the second threshold does *not* mean that someone understands Jesus, is convinced of his divinity, comprehends the cross, etc. It just means the person has become curious about Jesus or faith topics. And crossing that threshold is a wonderful miracle to celebrate.

Threshold #3: From being closed to change to becoming open to change. Many people have developed a trusting relationship with a Christian and even become quite interested in discussing faith topics but have never become Christians. There is, our friends have told us, a big difference between being a Jesus fan and actually being open to having Jesus change your life in some way. People who get stuck at this threshold are involved in a serious spiritual battle: so much in our flesh and in the spiritual realm makes us resistant to any kind of change in life. It is a significant spiritual breakthrough when someone's "Hey, I think Jesus is pretty fascinating!" becomes "I wonder if Jesus could help me improve my relationships. Maybe there's actually something I could get from this." We've found that unless someone is actually open to change, all our best apologetics and gospel presentations are falling on deaf (or happily content) ears.

Threshold #4: From meandering to seeking. Once people are open to change, they may begin to look for ways to incorporate

Jesus into areas of their life where they have holy discontent, but it does not necessarily follow that they will start a quest to come to ultimate answers and conclusions about Jesus. There is a big difference between meandering toward Jesus (genuine interest but no urgency) and seeking after ultimate answers. Someone who has crossed this threshold is on a quest to come to a conclusion about Jesus. This active seeking, this quest season, is actually quite exhausting to be in, and we've heard numerous stories of people who regressed backward in their journey if they weren't able to come to some solid conclusions. This is part of why recognizing when someone is at this threshold is so important.

Threshold #5: From lost to saved. For everyone who becomes a Christian there is a time (or season) when they start to follow Jesus. Whatever language you prefer to use (make a decision for Jesus, invite Jesus into their heart, become a Christian, convert, show evidence of regeneration, be born again), it's this final threshold that marks someone's "yes" to Jesus. Non-Christians don't necessarily know how to cross this threshold, which underscores how important it is that they have Christian friends helping them as they journey along.

Understanding where your friends are on their journey can help you discern how to best love them and help them. Our friends have told us, for example, that when they were at threshold #1 urgency from Christians was very off-putting and only dug the hole of distrust deeper. Patience and trust building were needed. But at threshold #5 it was helpful when Christian friends joined them in their urgency to come to a final decision about Jesus. Knowing where our friends are helps us love and serve them better. That's why the five thresholds have been so helpful to Christians.

Back to my (Doug's) small group in 1996. How do the insights of the five thresholds shed light on that thirty-week evangelistic gathering, which produced many amazing conversations about Jesus but not one person becoming a Jesus-follower? When I look at that group through the lens of the five thresholds, I realize that all those wonderful people who came faithfully to look at Jesus were not seekers, but were merely curious. They were not even open to personal change yet. At the time I did not know this about their process, nor did I know how to help them become open. They were unfortunately pretty much stuck at threshold #2.

THE WOMAN AT THE WELL

But is that process really unique to a postmodern journey? This is a fair question. On the one hand, it would appear that how people journey toward Jesus today is quite similar to how they have journeyed to faith for two thousand years. In John 4 we have the account of the woman who encounters Jesus in the heat of the day at the town's well—smack-dab in the middle of Samaria. We'll look at this story in greater depth later, but for now just consider the various steps this woman takes toward Jesus:

1. She naturally distrusts Jesus as a Jewish man. (Jesus builds trust by coming to her in her own setting, asking her—a Samaritan woman!—for a drink.)

2. She then asks Jesus a natural social question. (Jesus fans her curiosity by cryptically claiming to have "living water" she should be asking him for.)

3. She shows interest in the water but not in any kind of life change. (Jesus brings up the topic of the men in her life to get right at the discontent she is living with, to probe at an area of needed change.)

4. She doesn't run from Jesus when he implies change, but she does ask a detail question about where Samaritans and Jews are supposed to worship. She's trying to figure out Jesus and his claims. (Jesus honors her seeking by answering her question.)

5. She declares that when the Messiah comes, conclusions about all this will become clear. (Jesus prompts a sense of urgency by claiming to be the Messiah—she can come to conclusions then and there.)

This sure sounds similar to a lot of the conversion stories our friends have been telling us. So, on the one hand there is much that has not changed in how people journey to Jesus—and how to help them on that journey. On the other hand, there is something about our postmodern context that accentuates and affects how each threshold works and feels. The kind of distrust postmodern folks carry with them is quite different than what the woman at the well had. And it therefore needs to be addressed and handled differently. The kinds of questions postmodern folks are asking are very different from the woman's question about which mountain to worship on. And they therefore require very different answers.

MINISTERING IN A POSTMODERN CONTEXT

Our postmodern friends are journeying to Jesus in a way that is quite different than what their modern counterparts did in previous generations (see appendix A). This means the church needs to adapt and learn how to help them in their postmodern journey rather than blithely continuing to "do evangelism" in the modern way it's been done in the West for three hundred years. This is precisely where the uniquely postmodern features of the five thresholds are proving so helpful to Christians throughout the country as they genuinely wrestle with the two questions that are central to this ongoing conversation about evangelism:

- How do people come to Jesus in our postmodern context?
- How can Christians best help their friends on that journey?

Being a part of that conversation has been invigorating, enlightening, challenging, and humbling. It has brought us as students, teachers, trainers, and consultants into campus fellowships, mission organizations, evangelism movements, and numerous churches and denominations. And these experiences have forced all three of us to stare a third important question square in the face:

- How can whole communities become more fruitfully, joyfully, and regularly involved in helping people come to Jesus?

This community-oriented question has pushed us in the last few years beyond a mere personal application of the five thresholds (the primary focus of *I Once Was Lost*) to grapple with the community-wide implications of our postmodern context. What is possible for Christian communities in our postmodern context? Is it possible as leaders to help our communities grow as a whole in witnessing in this age?

During training sessions we've led on the five thresholds, participants move quickly from personal application questions (How do I tell where my friend is on their journey? How can I pique my friend's curiosity without seeming pushy? How do you help someone "cross the line" and become a Christian?) to more community-oriented questions. Some of the recurring questions we've heard are:

- I love the five thresholds, but how do I help my whole church understand all this?

- We have a few faithful evangelists, but for the most part our fellowship is fairly apathetic about evangelism. How do we change that?

- Is it really possible to change a church's witness temperature? Isn't it better to just plant a new church with evangelism built into its DNA?

- We're used to relying on events to share the gospel. How do we become a community that is building relationships and trust with non-Christians?

- We are seeing people come to faith every year now, but we remember a time when there were conversions every month! Is that still possible these days?

- We're seeing an increase in people coming to faith, but how do we disciple and incorporate them into our community?

- We want to be more of a witnessing community and are looking for our next pastor. What kinds of attributes should we be looking for?

- Do we need to completely change everything we're doing in order to become more relevant in this postmodern age?

While we have loved engaging these questions individually, we've seen great fruit in coming together to compare notes and wrestle through a more community-oriented application of the five thresholds. As the three of us have done that, two things have become clear to us. First, people are looking for solid answers to very practical questions about helping their community grow its witness. Second, the answers they need depend a lot on what kind of community they are leading.

THREE TYPES OF COMMUNITIES

Some Christian communities are almost completely unengaged in witness while others are joyfully active and purposeful in their witness. And many Christian communities are somewhere in between those two poles: they are engaged in witness on occasion but not necessarily aligned around witness all the time.

What leaders need to ask, do, pray for, strive after, change, and implement varies a lot depending on where their community is. What it looks like to lead a fairly indifferent witnessing community forward is very different than what it looks like to lead a somewhat witnessing community forward. While every community is unique in its own way (and presents its own unique leadership challenges), we've found that when it comes to witness, there are three basic types of communities that call for three different leadership responses (figure I.2).

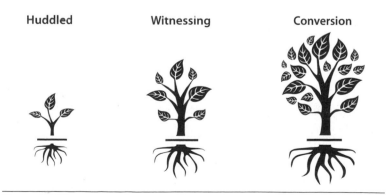

Figure I.2. Three types of communities

These three types of communities are pictured as different types of trees, for the following reasons. First, throughout the Bible God's people are likened to a tree, and the relative health of God's people is characterized as either a healthy and fruitful tree or an unhealthy and barren tree. We find this way of imaging God's people (and Christian communities) to be quite compelling when looking at the relative health of a community's witness. Second, while God is the ultimate author of salvation (we recognize that conversions are not something that can be controlled by humans), communities with healthier witness tend to see more people come to faith. There tends to be more evangelistic fruit. In this way, too, picturing trees that are more or less leafy and fruitful seems an apt way to characterize the three basic types of communities we've worked with over the years. Understanding what type of community you are in goes a long way in helping discern specific steps and strategies for growing your community's witness. So, what are the three basic types of communities when it comes to witness?

First, there are *huddled communities*. They have limited witness. These communities tend to look inward more than outward, and as a result, their concern for people inside the church often supersedes seeing and addressing needs of people outside the church. In these communities conversions are rare.

Other communities we work with have definitely (and explicitly) decided to be more outward focused. They are engaged in witness. They see witnessing as a key part of a Christian's discipleship and growth over time. It is normal in these communities to see multiple conversions every year. We call these *witnessing communities*.

Finally, some communities are comprehensively aligned around witness. They are filled with non-Christians throughout their events, folks who are relationally connected to the community through a friend. They tend to allow the Great Commission to shape all that they do, and it is normal to see adult conversions happening every month. Witnessing to Jesus is the "new normal" in their culture, saturating all they do. All the members talk about their faith with their non-Christian friends. We find it most clarifying and descriptive to call these *conversion communities*, for these reasons:[5]

- One of the most important observable distinctions between witnessing communities and conversion communities is how many people are becoming followers of Jesus for the first time.

- These conversions truly are conversions, and this regular influx of new faith and new life marks and even distinguishes these communities.

- Many communities do a lot of evangelistic activity and strive to grow their witness but do not make conversions their explicit goal. In this third type of community conversions are an explicit goal and explicitly prayed for.

Each type of witnessing community has its own habits and features, as shown in figure I.3. For example, if you were to visit five separate witnessing communities, they might look quite different from each other on the surface, but you might be surprised to discover that they tend to share similar habits and leadership challenges. It is the same with huddled communities; a great variety of churches and fellowships could be described as huddled, but they tend to share certain undeniable features with each other. This is what part one of *Breaking the Huddle* is all about.

Huddled	**Witnessing**	**Conversion**

Limited witness	*Engaged in witness*	*Aligned around witness*
• witness is a concept	• witness is a value	• witness shapes everything
• non-Christian presence in community is rare	• some non-Christians are involved in community	• many non-Christians involved in community
• conversions are rare	• multiple conversions annually	• multiple conversions monthly

Figure I.3. Characteristics of the three types of communities

In chapters one to three we will describe these three types of communities in detail, sharing stories and insights from the different huddled, witnessing, and conversion communities we have worked with over the years.

Understanding your own community is a key first step in helping it to grow. But understanding your community's current witness health is only the first step.

BREAKING THE HUDDLE

It is actually possible to help a community grow its witness: tepid huddled communities can learn to mobilize witnesses, and witnessing communities can become red-hot conversion communities (see figure I.4).

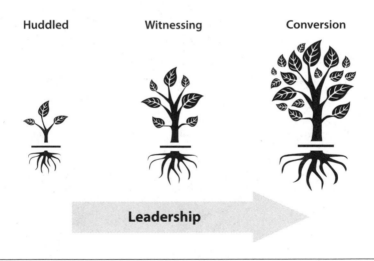

Huddled **Witnessing** **Conversion**

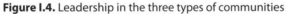

Leadership

Figure I.4. Leadership in the three types of communities

Is this kind of change easy? No way. In fact, over time there is a tendency for communities to wither in their witness. Left to themselves, witnessing communities will tend to regress back to being merely huddled; such is the reality of our flesh and our very real enemy. But the great news we have experienced firsthand is that it is possible for communities to grow their witness.

Just consider what happened to an InterVarsity community at the University of California San Diego (UCSD). Back in 2000, they were a very huddled community. They loved Jesus, they were devoted to digging deep in their lengthy Scripture studies, they had sincere prayer lives, they were passionate about urban ministry and serving the poor, they went to church faithfully, and they really enjoyed honest friendships with each other. They were a smart, sociable, passionate, huddled group of about two hundred members. Meanwhile, there were an additional 25,000 students on campus, most of whom had no experience of God's transforming love.

This huddled community had a powerful narrative about why this was the case. *People at UCSD are focused on science and too intellectual to be open to God. This is hard ground. The harvest is not ripe here. We are not good at evangelism—other communities are better at that. That is not our thing. We are focused on Scripture and serving the poor.* In fact, people would join InterVarsity for this very reason: they did not want to be challenged to make non-Christian friends. They did not want to be around the "E-word." For some of them *evangelism* was a dirty word. These members chose the huddle because they loved the feeling of the huddle.

UCSD was not the only huddled community in San Diego. As all the InterVarsity San Diego leaders looked at their ministries, they began to face the empirical facts. They were very honest with themselves: *Why are we so ineffective at helping those far from God become followers of Jesus? How come only two people became followers of Jesus through our ministry last year? That is just 1 percent of our whole group. That should bother us. Let's listen to God and see what he puts on our hearts.*

They wrestled with God over the internal question that plagued them as they looked at the facts and asked, *What's wrong with us? How did we let ourselves get so huddled?* They decided they needed to break the huddle. They decided to believe God for more. They shook off the old narrative that their context was simply not very open to God. This godly discontent was a profound turning point.

At UCSD, Megan, Ramiro, Ryan, and Serene formed a new team. Loving those far from God and investing in these new friendships became their top priority. They invited others from their community to join them. Very few did. But together they took risks. They failed. They learned. They had conflict with each other. They got new mentors. They prayed. Some other members of their huddled community accused them of turning their backs on their core values, like serving the poor and the oppressed and caring about God's heart of justice. This rift got worse, to the point that it threatened to split their community in two.

But Megan, Ramiro, Ryan, and Serene saw the change process through. They hung onto each other and onto the mission. They insisted on being aligned around witness, and God used this persistence and rugged faithfulness to indeed break the huddle. You might find it hard to believe what happened next.

If you visit InterVarsity at UCSD today, you would never guess they were once a huddled community. They have a thriving conversion community. For each of the past five years, they have helped over a hundred students *per year* become followers of Jesus. (This has tipped toward a whopping two hundred per year in the past two years.) Amazing! Today, no one says that people at UCSD simply are not very open to God. But it took a small community of four to begin to break the false narrative, to break the huddle.

Ryan, Ramiro, and Serene have each become leaders of this conversion movement. In addition, they now help inspire and equip other movement leaders across the country to believe God for more. To shake off the old narratives. To pray and go deeper with the Holy Spirit. And, ultimately, to break the huddle in their respective communities. In fact, several of the stories in this book come from conversion communities they have helped lead. (This is all the more amazing when you know that back in 2000, you would never have picked any of these folks out to be movement leaders.) God can use the most unlikely leaders and risk-takers to help a community break the huddle and grow its witness.

Ryan and UCSD's story has become for us a case study of what is possible. It is a story of hope for those of us who are still in the trial and error, depressive, head-banging-on-the-wall stage of trying to help a huddled community grow its witness. In short, Ryan, Ramiro, Megan, and Serene's story ought to give us hope that real change is possible. But this community is not alone. This is what truly gives us hope. We have seen God use a variety of teams, with a wide variety of temperaments and gifts, to help a community's witness grow over time. These stories form the backbone of *Breaking the Huddle.*

We'll introduce you to these communities, these leaders and more. The great news these testimonies point to is that real community-wide change is possible, and that purposeful (not magical) practical steps and influence and leadership can help make that change possible. A community really can grow its witness. Huddled communities can become witnessing communities. And witnessing communities can become conversion communities. While we keenly appreciate that every community is different, we have also become convinced that certain practical habits and strategies are typically helpful in a variety of contexts. There are real ways that we can help our communities grow their witness. But a couple caveats are in order.

Caveat #1. Does this mean that an increase in conversions is guaranteed? No. While it is possible for leaders to help their community grow its witness, and while this quite often corresponds to an increase in conversions, we cannot ultimately control conversions. No one can come to Jesus *unless the Father draws that person,* as Jesus put it (John 6:44). This doesn't release us from the exciting call to do all we can to help our community grow its witness, but it does release us from the heavy weight of eternal responsibility that we were never intended to shoulder.

Caveat #2. Is a healthy Christian community solely marked by being actively and fruitfully engaged in witness? No. God is shaping his people into vibrant communities that are engaged in sharing the good news—as well as living the good news, caring for the poor, comforting the sick and lonely, bringing reconciliation to those who are divided, enjoying the light of God's revealed Word, etc. In a sense, we've come to see witness as being a bit like kimchi, the wonderful, spicy Korean dish. It is marinated cabbage, a bit like sauerkraut. Kimchi isn't eaten on its own, but it makes the other parts of the meal more tasty. The same is true of evangelism: it is meant to be present throughout the robust life of a Christian community—not pitted against our other wonderful biblical values and practices but integrated with them.

Christ's body on earth is a stunningly beautiful thing. Witness is one part of that beauty. It is central to our calling as God's people and something that, without leadership, we tend to shy away from. That's why we've written this book.

When it comes to community-wide witness, leadership matters dearly. Leadership can keep a community's witness from withering. And (even more exciting) leadership can be used by God to grow a community's fruitfulness in witness. We really can be used by God in greater ways than we have in the past. By the end of *Breaking the Huddle* we hope you'll be just as inspired and equipped as we have been by learning from leaders who really are helping their communities grow in witness. That is our prayer for this book.

Since our own work and conversations have taken place in a variety of contexts, we have endeavored to include stories and illustrations from a wide variety of contexts as well. Whether you are in a church or a small group, a campus fellowship or a mission field, whether you are filled with hope or despairing as a leader, our hope is that this book will involve you right in the middle of the ongoing conversation about Christian witness in a postmodern context. For us this conversation, while exhausting at times, has filled us with genuine hope for God's mission on earth and for his chosen tool in that mission: his people.

In that sense, we hope that this book really helps us all break the huddle. Every athlete needs to take a knee for some time as she circles up with her teammates to figure out the next play. But then the team breaks the huddle and heads back out to the playing field. Breaking the huddle is an inherently hopeful, purposeful thing to do. May all our communities break the huddle and engage in the next play God has for us.

PRAYER

Father, please give me greater hope for what you can do in my community. Give me greater awareness that you are at work in the people around me. Give me discernment for where my friends, neighbors, and extended family are in their journey of moving toward you. Please have mercy on my community and on your worldwide church. Help us share Jesus with a hurting and broken world. Use this book to open my heart in new ways. Amen.

DISCUSSION

1. Where are you feeling inspired and hopeful about your community growing and changing?

2. Where are you feeling godly discontent? Where are you dissatisfied with your community?

As you pray, ask God to show you how he wants to transform you. Share with a friend. (For those who want concrete application in a small group, after reading each chapter see the online "Exercises and Activities for Getting Practical" for some specific growth steps. They can be found in the supplemental materials at ivpress.com/breaking-the-huddle.)

PART ONE

THREE TYPES OF
COMMUNITIES

1

HUDDLED COMMUNITIES

Limited Witness

A few years ago a Protestant denomination invited me (Don) to spend a couple days with pastors and key church leaders to help them think through how to become more engaged in evangelism. For decades the numbers of conversions in their churches had been flat, and the leaders were becoming discontent with this.

We met together in a church in Illinois in late winter, and I could tell that the pastors and leaders in the room were faithful, creative, passionate people. They clearly had a heart to be involved in front-line kingdom work and reach the communities where their churches were situated. A buzz of excitement and passion filled the room. But the atmosphere changed when I asked them to describe their congregations to me.

Their faces grew somber as they described how introverted and satisfied their congregations were. Many of their congregants had gone to church with each other for decades, and they all knew each other and loved their fellowship with each other. The pastors' love for these families was very clear, but so was their frustration as they described how rare it was to have anyone new involved in church activities and how long it had been since they had seen anything approaching a conversion. It was clear that most of these pastors were leading huddled congregations, and they couldn't shake the feeling that this wasn't as it was meant to be.

From the time Jesus began to build his church, he proclaimed that it would be beautiful, meaningful, and powerful—the "gates of hell" would not even prevail against it. A Christian community is a family of brothers and sisters united in Jesus, a place where those who are weary and heaven-laden come to find healing and hope, an instrument for world change as the light of the world. The church is Jesus' beloved bride.

But the unfortunate truth is that the bride isn't always in the best of health. Not every local church or Christian community is thriving. Some Christian communities can become, over time, more marked by division than unity, the cause of hurt rather than healing, and so insulated from the world around them that one might be tempted to describe them as a light that's been hidden under a bowl. Of course, as Jesus reminded his disciples, no one lights a lamp and then hides it under a bowl. That'd be ridiculous! But it's not so rare among Christian communities. These are huddled communities (figure 1.1).

Huddled	Witnessing	Conversion

Limited witness
- witness is a concept
- non-Christian presence in community is rare
- conversions are rare

Figure 1.1. Three stages of witnessing communities

A huddled community is exactly what it sounds like: a Christian community that is, for the most part, insulated from the world around them. Huddled communities vary greatly in size and culture and worship style, but they share one feature: they have little impact on the people and world around them. And for the most part, they are fine with that.

In a huddled community, having deep relationships with people outside the church is not necessarily a high value, and conversions are rare. This may sound sad, but there are real distinct advantages that come from being in a huddled community: it feels safe, it is familiar, and it works. There can be a great and robust sense of "belonging" that comes for those who are in the community—people know your name, and you know those around you. You know what to expect.

There are several types of huddled communities:

- *Declining.* Some huddled communities are timid and shy by nature. Think of a small church that is just getting by, keeping the doors open, perhaps reminiscing about better days gone by.

- *Intimate.* Some huddled communities are intimate and transformative. Think of a community where discipleship and healing are greatly emphasized, where everyone knows each other—and they like it that way.

- *Intense.* Other huddled communities are aggressive and vision-oriented. Think of an energized military-like community that is captivated by and centered around careful doctrinal preaching and teaching.

- *Defensive.* Some churches view the secular world around them as a threat to their own health and faithfulness (and that of their children), and a purposeful distance is kept from outsiders; the insularity of the church is purposefully maintained and seen as a virtue.

- *Country club.* Still other huddled communities can function like a social club. Think of a large, traditional, steepled church where significant members of the community have always been expected to congregate and network, a place where people go to church because of social or familial expectations.

This last kind of huddled community is what Bonhomme Presbyterian Church used to be like. I (Don) have been at Bonhomme since 2008 but have heard stories about what it was like in the 1980s. The church has a long and varied history beginning in 1816, but in the 1980s it was known in the community as a country club church. Anyone who was anyone in the West County area of St. Louis came: politicians, professional athletes, successful business people. Bonhomme was a place to see and be seen.

While there was definitely a sense of energy and excitement, the church community tended to be huddled by nature. The irony is somewhat palpable because the church was founded by a missionary pastor who rode on a horse from Connecticut to Missouri during the depths of winter to reach out and plant it. The church's self-description at the time, "Bonhomme: a light on a hill," may have been geographically accurate (it is situated on one of the highest hills in West County St. Louis), but spiritually this wasn't quite the case for the church as a whole. Jesus may have concluded that "a light on a hill cannot be hidden," but from a kingdom perspective Bonhomme's light was pretty well covered up by the busyness and distractions of the social environment.

This doesn't mean nothing of value was happening at Bonhomme, but it does mean that, on the whole, the church's evangelistic temperature was very cool. Bearing witness to the good news was not a high priority and conversions were very rare. Bonhomme was a huddled community.

Of course, there is nothing new about these huddled dynamics. Even Jesus himself had to deal with huddled tendencies in his own disciples.

JOHN 4: THE DISCIPLES AND THEIR LUNCH

We've already visited the well outside a village in Samaria where Jesus stopped to rest while his disciples went into a nearby city for food. That well was the site of a fascinating, sensitive interaction between Jesus and a woman from the village. Last time we visited that well we focused on Jesus and his interactions with the woman, but consider for a moment the posture of his disciples that day.

The context is important, of course. Jews at the time would not have traveled through Samaria, and the Samaritans were just fine with that. John just tells us that Jesus "had to go through Samaria" without divulging his exact motivation. Not only was the Samaritan woman taken aback by Jesus' presence in Samaria and his willingness to interact with her, but so were Jesus' disciples. John puts it this way: "Just then his disciples came back. They marveled that he was talking with a woman, but no one said, 'What do you seek?' or, 'Why are you talking with her?'" (John 4:27 ESV).

Whereas Jesus' instinct was to reach out, build trust, and arouse curiosity, his disciples' instincts were to gape. Is it because Jesus is interacting with a Samaritan? Because she is a woman? Because she might be an outcast in her village? We don't know precisely, but we do know that there are several social layers isolating the disciples from this woman. It would be normal and expected for them *not* to interact with her, and they are fine with that. So Jesus' act of reaching out through those layers is something that makes them gape.

It is also noteworthy that while the disciples weren't willing to say anything to Jesus about this untoward reaching out he's done, they *are* willing to talk about food. John (who was there that day) makes it clear how ironic and small-minded their questions about food were.

> So the woman left her water jar and went away into town and said to the people, "Come, see a man who told me all that I ever did. Can this be the Christ?" They went out of the town and were coming to him. Meanwhile the disciples were urging him, saying, "Rabbi, eat." But he said to them, "I have food to eat that you do not know about." So the disciples said to one another, "Has anyone brought him something to eat?" Jesus said to them, "My food is to do the will of him who sent me

and to accomplish his work. Do you not say, 'There are yet four months, then comes the harvest'? Look, I tell you, lift up your eyes, and see that the fields are white for harvest." (John 4:28-35 ESV)

Looking back John realizes how blind he and the other disciples had been to the great kingdom happenings (the entire village making their way out to find Jesus) and how fixated they were on their own appetites (everything was about food for them that day). Jesus' eyes were on the fields that were ripe for harvest, while theirs were on the food on their laps. Jesus was preoccupied with doing God's will in spreading the Word that day. They were preoccupied with their bellies. John underscores this contrast in the text.

Those who are fed up with their huddled Christian community can perhaps take comfort from the fact that Jesus himself had to reckon with his disciples' isolationist tendencies. We're not alone in this dilemma. While it is instructive to note how Jesus calls his disciples out of their isolation (which we will get to later), it is also meaningful to pause here and parse out some of the habits and temptations that people in huddled communities tend to have.

THE THREE HABITS OF A HUDDLED COMMUNITY

Sitting around a well with Jesus isn't exactly the same as the life of a local church or Christian community, but the same instincts that were present in the disciples that day in Samaria tend to be present in some form in huddled communities. Most huddled communities tend to

- focus on their own needs,

- fail to prioritize relationships with "outsiders," and

- view evangelism as special.

Huddled communities focus on their own needs. John doesn't seem to be critiquing his and the other eleven disciples' need to eat food that day in Samaria (there is something quite unavoidable about feeding our bellies!), but he does seem to be lamenting how preoccupied they were with food—rather than being more attentive to the kingdom work that was going on. They go off to get food (while Jesus reaches out to this needy woman), they urge Jesus to eat (when he's gazing over their heads at the curious villagers approaching), and they wonder if someone else has given him something to eat (when he speaks of the "food" of doing God's will).

Today huddled communities can have the same habit. They can become so preoccupied with their own needs and appetites that they can't see much else. A kind of tunnel vision can set in where their entire field of view is taken up with their own needs and problems and hungers. With this tunnel vision comes a real sense of urgency about problems or issues that (in the big picture) might be really minor or petty. There's something about having limited horizons that makes everything right around you appear to be monumental and important, even if in reality it is relatively insignificant.

It is amazing how much passion people can muster over mundane things. We know a pastor of a church that was contemplating repainting the sanctuary. Now aesthetics are an important part of hospitality and thought should always be put into such details, but a firestorm of drama erupted over which shade of a particular color was to be used. The Paint Drama became so impassioned that one member declared that she was going to leave the church if a certain shade was not chosen! And she was most definitely not kidding.

This may seem outrageous or even comical, but it is a reliable feature in almost every huddled community. One might think that being insulated would drain a church of passion and drama and urgency, but in practice people just get passionately focused on internal needs in an unhealthy and imbalanced way. Over time this has two effects on the huddled community: (1) there is an *appearance* of real dramatic church activity, and (2) internal needs take on an exaggerated scale of importance and urgency. This can make a community even more fearful or suspicious of trying to grow their witness. *How can we start a new outreach to others when the warranty on the furnace just expired? How can we think about serving outside our church community when the prayer list for our own community multiplies each day?*

I (Don) wasn't at Bonhomme in the '80s, but I've been assured that the Session's minutes (a detailed monthly record of the major decisions, debates, and efforts of the church) from that time are just as full as in any other decade. It can be quite exciting, engaging, and even exhausting to focus on our own needs. But most huddled communities we've worked with don't just focus on their own needs; they also tend to avoid deep relationships with "outsiders."

Huddled communities fail to prioritize relationships with "outsiders." None of the disciples were brave enough that day in Samaria to speak their heart, but John tells us what they were all thinking when they came back and found Jesus talking to a Samaritan (gasp!) who happened to be a woman (gasp!) who was probably an outcast in her village (gasp!). They were thinking: *What is Jesus doing talking with that woman?!* Granted, this was early in their discipleship journey, but apparently Jesus' other-oriented posture was still limited (at least in their minds) to certain people. There was no way he should be talking to *her*.

While Jesus would eventually get very explicit that he was sending his disciples to everyone—Jerusalem, Judea, Samaria, and the ends of the earth—this story reveals how isolationist we can be. Even as Christians. (Perhaps *especially* as Christians?) This is a feature of huddled communities we've noticed again and again: they purposefully avoid deep relationships with "outsiders." A deep relationship doesn't necessarily imply being best friends or constantly intimate with each other, but it does imply a relationship in which two people know each other enough to genuinely trust each other. Trust, as we saw in the introduction, is a key element in relational witness. In huddled communities these kinds of trusting relationships with non-Christians don't tend to be common.

When we do training on the five thresholds we often ask people to identify the two non-Christians they are closest to and think about them through the framework of the five thresholds. Which threshold would they say their non-Christian friend is at? It's a very helpful exercise to keep the learning about the thresholds from being purely academic.

But what happens when we do this exercise in a community that turns out to be a mostly huddled community? It grinds to a halt at this humbling, almost embarrassing realization: they aren't in a close relationship with a single non-Christian. While this realization can be painful, the causes of this situation can be numerous. We've rarely met a group of antisocial Christians who have explicitly decided to avoid contact with others, but we have seen a variety of reasons why individual Christians (and even whole communities) avoid investing in trusting and meaningful relationships with "outsiders" over time.

Busyness: "I'm just so busy." Some folks are so busy going to church meetings, meeting with church folks, and planning church events that they have no relational bandwidth for the non-Christians around them. Relationships of depth take time. They take presence. And if most of our time and presence are taken up with other Christians, it's not too surprising that no real relationships with non-Christians are taking root in our lives.

Protectiveness: "We don't want to be tempted." Sometimes we huddle with others because we are afraid of what is outside the huddle. The huddle is safe and gives us a sense of security. For those with budding faith, a huddle can be a life-giving space to make lifestyle decisions. We can imagine the disciples liking their huddle with Jesus, but Jesus was always bringing people into that cozy little huddle. Just as the disciples saw Samaria as a "dirty" place where they could be spiritually tainted, many Christians view the secular world and normal people as "icky" and to be avoided at all costs. In our zeal for holiness we can grow more and more allergic to rubbing shoulders with non-Christians. We remember Jesus' injunction not to be "of the world," but we forget what he said about being sent "into the world" (see John 17:14-19). Where limiting contact with non-Christians is viewed as a virtue, it is understandable why deep relationships with outsiders is so rare.

Avoidance: "It's just hard to be around those people." There's no use pretending the disciples didn't have an inbred cultural distaste for all things Samaritan. And there's no use pretending that as Christians we don't have some fear, anger, superiority, and apathy toward some of the groups of people around us. We do. We just plain do. There can be something about non-Christians' language or politics or shallowness or crassness or *whatever* that just makes us feel uncomfortable. And sometimes that's why we avoid relationships with others. *I have a problem with those people who . . .* (fill in the blank). Prejudice is like a pesticide that prevents trusting relationships with others from naturally taking root, growing, and blossoming. Prejudice is often very difficult to see in ourselves, not to mention addressing it as a whole community.

Volunteering: "We are already doing a lot of outreach." There are churches that see themselves as very active in "outreach" but don't have real, deep relationships with people outside the church. Volunteering at a soup kitchen is a wonderful kingdom activity, but it doesn't necessarily involve building relationships with people outside your church, let alone deep relationships. At times such wonderful volunteering can make people think they are "outreach oriented," which can dull any felt need to develop relationships with others. Net result: a church may feel very outreach oriented but trust and relationships with others are not being developed. (If this volunteering describes your outreach, you might do well to change the name of your outreach committee to a mercy ministry committee.) It may seem ironic, but our busy volunteering can cause us to avoid deep relationships with the non-Christians living right next door to us.

Pastors: "The ones I look up to are always in the huddle." For many of us the people we look up to the most, who model the Christian faith for us the most, whose stories of faithfulness we hear the most are our pastors. The three of us are huge fans of pastors (Don is an ordained Presbyterian pastor), but our leaders can unintentionally stunt our relational life with non-Christians by not modeling relationship building with people who don't come to church. Like it or not, one of the vocational hazards that comes with being a pastor or minister is that you are working with Christians all the time. As

Christian leaders we know how tempting it is to fill all of your hours and days with relationships with Christians. The one who stands up and preaches and teaches and gives a life picture of what it means to follow Jesus is someone who spends all their time drinking coffee with other Christians. This can have the subtle effect, over time, of nurturing a Christian community that does not develop relationships with non-Christians. (It wouldn't hurt if pastors also changed their language from the pulpit, and instead of referring to others as "outsiders," used words like "those who are curious" or "seekers" to help warm our hearts in a positive direction.)

So for a wide variety of reasons, some people avoid the unhurried, beautiful task of building relationships with non-Christians. The result can be that we just don't have relationships with non-Christians, and whole churches can find themselves in a very huddled state. This is important to recognize and name because in our postmodern context it is very difficult to share the gospel without relationships. The gospel wants to be shared in the warm light of a relationship.

Huddled communities view evangelism as special. Some may avoid the topic of witness and evangelism altogether, but almost every huddled community (when they do think of evangelism) tends to view it as a very special activity. This may seem like the recipe for a high evangelism temperature—if it's seen as "special," doesn't that turn up the sense of urgency and importance of evangelism? But in reality the more "special" evangelism seems to a community, the less evangelism is a part of their everyday life.

How exactly do whole communities treat evangelism as special? And how does that tend to keep their evangelistic temperature so low? Folks in huddled communities tend to believe a few specific things about evangelism:

- *Evangelism is better left to professionals.* It is tremendous that God has gifted certain individuals for a lifetime ministry of evangelism, but the unintended message can be that sharing the faith is something that only specially gifted, anointed Christians are called to do. It may seem an overstatement, but in practice many Christians are operating under the assumption that sharing the faith is something for the Billy Grahams and Luis Palaus of the world, not for them. The irony is that many huddled communities actually have a great deal of respect for evangelism and evangelists. They just don't see it as something that intersects with their own life of faith in a significant way. Evangelism is revered as a special game in which they are not players.

- *Evangelism is for special times.* It is seen as something that doesn't take place in the warp and woof of everyday life but only on special days and times that are marked on the calendar. This may seem counterintuitive, but sometimes holding evangelistic events sends the unintended, perhaps subconscious, message that evangelism happens solely through events and not through relationships. And, sadly, sometimes our busyness with an event actually has the effect of dulling any real urgency to slowly build relationships with a few non-Christians in our lives. After all, because of events, we can see ourselves as active witnesses (putting up signs, advertising, mixing up a large batch of lemonade, bringing in an evangelistic speaker, having an altar call—think of all that activity!), but at the same time we can be passive relationship builders. (Note: Can God use events to bring people to faith? Absolutely. Do some events make it easier for us to build relationships with non-Christians in our lives? Absolutely. Does holding an event make your community automatically nonhuddled? Nope. Plenty of huddled communities hold evangelistic events.) If evangelism is seen as only occurring at special times and places, then Christians tend not to be about the slow, unglamorous, everyday business of building relationships with non-Christians.

- *Evangelism means being a know-it-all.* Some Christians assume that engaging in evangelism means having all the answers. This can make evangelism seem intimidating: *What if they ask me a question I don't know the answer to? What if I tell them something wrong? What if they find out what an imperfect Christian I am? What if they know more about the Bible than I do? I hate when evangelism turns into arguments with my friends.* Rather than facing these assumptions and working through them in prayer and conversation, folks in huddled communities can become passive in their witness, missing out on what God might be doing around them.

If you can relate to one or more of the above, I (Val) am with you. I have struggled with a number of these barriers and huddled habits over the years. Because I did not see evangelism as a primary gift of mine, I often left evangelism to the people I thought were more gifted than I was. I would hide behind my other gifts and tell myself that evangelism is better left to others.

In part I did this because I didn't want my lack of evangelism skills to be exposed to friends in my community. I struggled with self-doubt. I also prided myself on not being a know-it-all. To be honest, I passed judgment on people who did argumentative evangelism. I told myself, *I'm glad I'm not like those irritating people.* I used this as an excuse not to get better at evangelism.

Part of God's invitation to me was to admit out loud to my friends that I was stuck in huddled thinking and living. Another part of my repentance was the decision to intentionally ask questions of those I viewed as gifted in evangelism to learn from them and to help me name the skills I needed to develop. In my own life I've learned it's possible for a huddled Christian to grow in witness. In my ministry I've learned this is possible for whole communities.

THE REALITY AND HOPE OF BEING IN (AND EVEN LEADING) A HUDDLED COMMUNITY

It can be mighty frustrating to wake up one day and realize that you are a part of a huddled community, especially if you long to see the community grow its witness (see figure 1.2). It can be downright embarrassing if you are in a position of leadership—*I thought we were doing pretty well, but when it comes right down to it I have to admit our witness temperature is low, conversions are rare, and we exhibit parts of each of these habits. How does that reflect on me as the leader?* It can be frustrating—*I've been trying everything I know to do, but folks just aren't responding. I feel like I'm beating my head against a wall.* And it can be complicated—*I was hired at this church because they wanted to grow in their witness, but they seem to resist every change I introduce. We took such great steps forward two years ago, but now things seem so flat and huddled again. I thought I was asked to become an elder because of my passion for evangelism, but I don't feel like anyone is listening to me.*

While it can be frustrating to realize you are in a huddled community, that frustration is actually a blessing. It might just be a sign of godly discontentment—a holy desire to see your community grow in witness. Frustration is oftentimes a wonderful alternative to complacency. If you are part of (or even leading) a huddled community and are frustrated with the status quo, it is important to acknowledge head-on some of the realities that come with helping your community grow its witness.

Huddled Communities

Limited witness

- witness is a concept
- non-Christian presence in community is rare
- conversions are rare

Habits:

1. focus on own needs
2. avoid deep relationships with outsiders
3. view witness as special

Figure 1.2. Habits of huddled communities

First, it takes time. The vibrancy of a community's witness is not going to go from a barren tree to a fruitful orchard overnight. Just consider Jesus' own process of forming and shepherding and equipping his own disciples. John 4 is a wonderful case study. John's record of the events by that well is not only a testament to how good and loving Jesus was with the Samaritan woman but also to how patient Jesus was with his own disciples. The gospel of Mark, as a whole, is a tremendous record of the disciples' bumbling, blindness, pride, huddled tendencies, and resistance to change. If it took Jesus himself time to shape a community, should we expect any less for us? If the twelve disciples were huddled by nature, should we be surprised to find that same inertia within our own hearts and communities? The reality is that leading a huddled community toward change takes time.

It also takes love. Many leaders who were fed up with their communities have contacted us over the years. It can be maddening to shepherd a huddled community (especially if you are discontent with the insularity), and our love can be slowly replaced with frustration, anger, incredulity, and apathy. But it takes real love and empathy to shepherd a huddled community. It may be unhealthy for a church to be focused on their own needs, but that doesn't mean those needs aren't real or that the people don't really care about them. It may be unhealthy to avoid deep relationships with outsiders, but that doesn't mean deep relationships within the church are bad. Here Jesus is such a beautiful model for us. Read the Gospel of Mark from start to finish and you want to jump into the pages and shake the shoulders of the frustratingly dull disciples! But what does Jesus do? He loves them. He definitely leads them and develops them, but with great care and empathy and amazing patience. It is difficult to lead a huddled community for the long haul without love. We do not suggest doing it.

Leadership is difficult, and leading a huddled community is no different. Leading such a church or community does involve particular challenges, but it would be a mistake to leave such a post assuming that your next leadership task will be devoid of challenges and frustrations. This is why it's important to also recognize and celebrate the hope of leading a huddled community.

REDEEMING HUDDLES

The hope is this: Christian huddles have a way of turning into amazing plays. We may decry the "holy huddle," but let's extend the American football analogy. Teams get into a huddle in order to do what? Prepare for the next play! The players face each other in a tight circle before each play. The other team cannot enter. They need this private space to get crystal clear on the next play. They have to be close enough to tune out the crowd and hear the quarterback call the play. This is how they become single-minded, which is key to success. There is also camaraderie in the huddle. They regroup, they focus, they keep the momentum going.

In that sense, a Christian "huddle" is a good thing: it allows us to develop camaraderie and unity, it helps us focus on the next "play"— what God's Word calls us to be about and to do—and it allows our God-appointed leaders an opportunity to speak to us and guide us as a whole group. Huddled communities have this going for them: they are circled up! They are together. Christian community can be similar to a football huddle. We huddle together because we yearn to be with people who understand and think like us. We need other Christians for joy, vision, community, and guidance to keep walking the faith journey. There is camaraderie and shared motivation and practical help to keep moving forward in our quest to know Jesus and become more like him.

Jesus himself had many huddled moments with his disciples. He created private conversations. They needed to hear the inside scoop about what Jesus was thinking. They needed *some alone time with their Master*. The huddle was designed for us Christians to get what we need from God and each other so that we can better fulfill the Great Commission Jesus gave us, "to go and make disciples."

And that's where "breaking the huddle" comes in. Wouldn't it be odd if a football team stayed in their huddle forever on the field? The referees would come over and remind the team that they are there to play the game! So they need to break their huddle and play.

The challenge in huddled communities is that the scope and purpose of the huddle may have gotten lost along the way. The huddle that was designed for vision, clarity, and guidance to keep moving toward the mission God gave us as believers has become *the* mission. We mistake Christian community as the mission versus the Great Commission as the mission.

But the great hope of leading a huddled community is that God's people have within their spiritual DNA a pulsing desire to live out the kingdom of God, to be about God's mission. Jesus told his disciples that they were the salt of the earth and the light of the world. (He didn't say "try to be like" salt and light!) By virtue of following him they were becoming inherently purposeful and redemptive. "You *are* my witnesses," Jesus proclaimed over his church. And he sent his Holy Spirit to empower it and guide it forward in that witnessing mission.

What exactly does it mean to be a witness (and by extension, a witnessing community)? First, it means that you've seen something. Second, it means that you tell others about what you've seen. This simple twofold framework of both seeing and saying can be a really helpful way for a community to diagnose their witness. Are they really seeing God at work? And are they saying things to others about it? That's what it means to be a witness.

This is the great hope of leading a huddled community: they are God's people. His Spirit is within them. His Son Jesus is the head of the church, its controlling and coordinating mechanism. We have, implicitly, seen something: God at work in history, inside us, and around us. While our flesh and temptations and group inertia and the enemy's lies may impede our mission for a time, that mission is inside of us, embedded in the hearts of Christians. And as we see in the New Testament, God has chosen to use imperfect human leaders to guide, shepherd, love, and convict his beautiful church forward on her mission.

That's exactly what happened at Bonhomme in the 1990s. One of the leaders, Suzy Gaeddert, had a heart for evangelism and wanted to see her church grow its own witness. But Bonhomme was fairly huddled. So what did Suzy do? She invited all the church's leadership to huddle up together and take the Alpha course.[1] In this way she brought God's passion for the lost (which is what Alpha is all about) into the huddle of leaders. God used this leadership huddle to "call the next play," and thus was launched a decade of increasing witness. Bonhomme became a community with excited witnesses, a community that included non-Christians and that saw multiple conversions every year. This is the hope of being a part of a huddled community—ultimately it's a community that belongs to God, and God has a way of shepherding his people forward.

If, like that group of pastors Don met with in Illinois, you ever feel frustrated by your community or your tough context, spend some time reading Acts as a whole. This new, imperfect, ragtag church is called to be God's witnesses "in Jerusalem, and in all Judea and Samaria, and to the ends of the earth" (Acts 1:8). And along the way they lock themselves away in upper rooms, face tremendous internal obstacles, and experience a level of external resistance that few of us can even imagine. And yet.

And yet what is the message of Acts? Christ's church moves forward. No one can stop her. Not even the gates of hell can stop her. Not her own temptations, not the enemy, not the flesh, not group inertia, not prison, not martyrdom. Nothing. What is the final word of the book of Acts? The last ringing note that comes from this action-adventure book of the Bible is *unhindered*. Paul "proclaimed the kingdom of God and taught about the Lord Jesus Christ—with all boldness and without hindrance!" (Acts 28:31). The gospel is going forward *unhindered*. Such is the hope embedded in the church still to this day.

PRAYER

Father, I am a busy person. I do not feel very gifted at evangelism. I don't like feeling awkward. I prefer to be around people who share my Christian values and lifestyle. Please open my heart to try new things. Please grow in me a heart of courage and love for those who do not yet know you. I give you permission to transform me. The same is true for my community. We give you permission to transform us. Holy Spirit, use us more and more to show your love and power to those far from you. Amen.

DISCUSSION

1. Which type of huddled community might describe us?
   - the declining huddled church
   - the intimate huddled church

- the intense huddled church
- the defensive huddled church
- the country club huddled church

2. All communities may struggle with the five barriers to witness. Discuss where you see these in yourself personally and in your community.

   - busyness: *"I'm just so busy."*
   - protectiveness: *"We don't want to be tempted."*
   - avoidance: *"It's just hard to be around those people."*
   - volunteering: *"We are already doing a lot of outreach."*
   - pastors: *"The ones I look up to are always in the huddle."*

3. Which of these habits does our community struggle with the most? Why?

   - focusing on our own needs
   - avoiding deep relationships with "outsiders"
   - viewing evangelism as special

4. What is one next step you want to take to help your community break the huddle?

HOW TO CREATE A PRAYER MAP

One way of fighting against the tendency to huddle is to regularly pray for non-Christians around you. A helpful step toward that end is the creation of a personal prayer map (see figure 1.3). These prayer maps are a helpful way to identify the people whom God has put in our lives.

- Write down three to four networks (work, neighborhood, family, etc.) where you have friends. Then write a few names around each network.

- Pray: *God, please bring to mind the name of one person who does not know your love.*

- Turn to your neighbor. Pray for each other, for the friend whom God brought to mind, and for an opportunity to build more trust this week.

- Debrief one week later: From your prayer map, with whom did you try to build trust? What did you do? What did you learn about yourself?

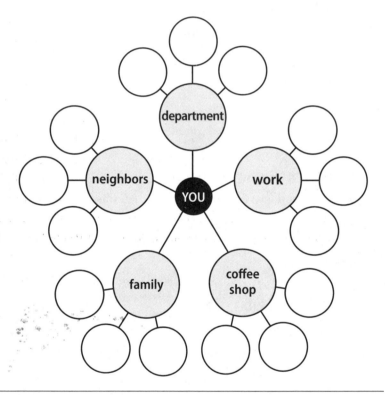

Figure 1.3. Prayer map

2

WITNESSING COMMUNITIES

Engaged in Witness

We had no idea at Bonhomme Presbyterian Church what God would do through that first Alpha course. Members of the church began, some for the first time in their lives, to care about sharing Jesus with others. The value of witnessing was lifted up and celebrated by the church (in announcements, sermons, etc.), there was a helpful structure to facilitate relational evangelism (multiple Alpha courses were run each year), and a cohort of people within the church genuinely began to see themselves as playing a role in helping people discover Jesus.

Looking back, it is clear that this community had broken the huddle. The leaders taking Alpha together functioned as a team huddle that brought the group together to focus on the next play: God wanting to reach the community around them. When that first course ended, they broke the huddle with renewed purpose, vision, and willingness to play the game.

Soon the real excitement began. Lifelong Christians were being refreshed in their faith, and a few non-Christians came to faith for the first time. God was active, doing something in this previously huddled community. Nothing unifies, inspires, and mobilizes a

Christian community like seeing God move. *Really* seeing God *really* move.

When God shows up and works, his people are right to take note and marvel at what he has done. God's people can't help but praise him when they see him heal someone, reconcile enemies, humble a proud person, or draw a lost and hurting soul into his kingdom. In fact, a chorus of marveling at these moments of God's work fills the pages of Scripture. As we have it in the Psalms, "Glad songs of salvation are in the tents of the righteous: 'The right hand of the LORD does valiantly, the right hand of the LORD exalts, the right hand of the LORD does valiantly!'" (Psalm 118:15-16 ESV). God's "right hand" is a phrase used to celebrate a distinct moment when God has been at work among his people.

Many Christian communities today welcome such moments of God being at work. In relation to witness, there are those who not only expect God moments in their own Christian community but also expect God to be at work in the non-Christians around them. They expect to see God's "right hand" valiantly bringing lost people home to his kingdom. In such communities Christians are prayerfully

Huddled	Witnessing	Conversion

Limited witness	*Engaged in witness*	
• witness is a concept	• witness is a value	
• non-Christian presence in community is rare	• some non-Christians are involved in community	
• conversions are rare	• multiple conversions annually	

Figure 2.1. Characteristics of witnessing communities

expectant, looking to see where God is at work. And they tend to be *active* partners with God, gladly helping their friends as they journey toward Jesus, walking with those who are seeking, praying with those who want more, helping people respond to God's work in their lives. These are what we call "witnessing communities" (figure 2.1).

WITNESSING COMMUNITIES

A witnessing community has a fairly warm witness temperature. Helping other people in their journey toward Jesus is seen as a normal part of what it means to be a follower of Jesus. Witnessing communities have heard and responded to the call of God to be a blessing to others. This isn't just a corporate endeavor and value (holding large evangelistic events, for example) but is part of the heartbeat of the members of the community. People see themselves as individually engaged with the non-Christians in their own social circles.

Not only do these communities assume that being a witness is a normal part of what it means to be a Christian, but they incorporate this assumption into their teaching, their discipleship structures, and even their programming and budgets. They assume God is seeking out people in their midst and endeavor to partner with him in that mission.

Some of these witnessing communities are very big: think of a church of twelve hundred that has an active congregation, creates special events for non-Christians, has regular altar calls, and sees dozens of conversions a year. Some of these communities are small: think of a church of one hundred active, invitational members who have turned the coffee hour after church into a vibrant place of hospitality and relationship building and sees two to five people come to faith a year.

Other witnessing communities aren't churches at all but vibrant groups of Christians: think of a fellowship of fifty students on a state campus who are so enjoying life in Jesus that they have become a magnet for students who are curious about their joyful fellowship. These students receive regular training on how to journey with a friend who is spiritually seeking, and their group has seen about four folks commit their lives to Jesus every year for the last three years. Or think of a small group of Christians who have placed hospitality and conversation with non-Christians as a high value and regularly inhabit a coffee shop where they are building real relationships and helping people get to know Jesus over time.

Other witnessing communities can be vibrant pockets within larger, more huddled communities: think of a youth group filled with students who have a heart for their fellow students and regularly invite friends to youth group events and retreats and see several of these friends discover Jesus for the first time. All that happens within a larger church body that may be quite huddled as a whole. Or think of an outreach team that has been serving in the same mercy ministry in the city for years, developing many relationships with non-Christians, even though their larger church remains relatively huddled.

Though witnessing communities can look quite different, we've noticed a number of features they all seem to have in common:

- They have an explicit vision to be about sharing the gospel with others.

- They expect God to be at work in their midst and are on the lookout for God moments.

- It is normal to have non-Christians in the mix at community events and services.

- Community members are receiving some sort of training, encouragement, and motivation to be a witness.

- Structures, programs, and language from up front seem to take into account the possibility that some folks in the room are exploring faith.

- Testimonies of life change (and conversion) are told and celebrated.

- The number of folks who are coming to faith each year is about 2 to 5 percent of the size of the whole group (about two to five adult conversions on average for every one hundred active members of the group).

Truro Anglican Church in Fairfax, Virginia, is one such community. The Truro parish has been around since 1732. It's a historic, steepled church that counts George Washington as a one-time member of the leadership vestry, and famous Civil War events occurred in buildings on their campus. Truro may not be what most people envision when they are asked to picture a vibrant Christian community involved in witness, but that's exactly what it is.

Relational evangelism is a high value at Truro: you can't visit their website or one of their services without getting the sense that Truro is about sharing Jesus with others. Truro has adopted the Alpha course as their strategic model for empowering members of the church to do relational witness. There is always an Alpha course going in English or Spanish, or an Alpha marriage or parenting course. Evangelism training is provided for leaders and members of the congregation. During Sunday worship it is assumed that new people are in attendance, and a hospitable tone is taken in welcoming them and inviting them to take next steps. Community-wide events are held that provide a safe first step into the life of the church—like their annual Carols by Glowstick, a fun event for folks of all ages to sing familiar Christmas carols while waving and playing with hundreds of glow sticks.

The stories of life change and conversion at Truro are joyful and common. There are God moments happening throughout the life of the church, and space is made to recognize those moments and respond to them. For example, it is assumed that God might be doing a special work in someone's life during worship, so time is set aside for unhurried prayer during worship.

While Truro has a fascinating and long history, folks there are more concerned with what God's right hand is doing in their own time. They are on the lookout for God moments and respond joyfully to them when they happen. Of course, there is nothing new about recognizing and responding to a God moment. This is, in a sense, exactly what happened when Jesus sat down at that well in Samaria.

JOHN 4: JESUS AND THE TIME AT THE WELL

This is another lesson we learn from the encounter with the Samaritan woman at the well: Jesus was attentive to the God moment he was in and willing to respond to that moment.

Jesus was clearly tired and looking for rest, yet he recognized that this was potentially a special moment for this woman. Not just a happenstance encounter at a well but a real God moment. It would seem Jesus could tell the difference between normal time and appointed moments. Jesus embraced the moment and actively engaged with this woman. This is precisely the kind of posture Paul encouraged the believers in Ephesus to mirror when he encouraged them to be "making the best use of the time" (Ephesians 5:16 ESV). Of the two words for "time" in the Greek available to him, Paul here used *kairos* (an appointed moment) rather than the more pedestrian *chronos* (simple passage of time). Paul is encouraging Christians to do exactly what Jesus did: make the most of the appointed moment in front of them—a potential God moment.

But the disciples? They too were tired, and we know that they were hungry. They seem rather put out by this woman's presence and Jesus' engagement with her. They don't recognize the special God moment that is happening and therefore lean back from it with their arms crossed (emotionally if not also physically) while Jesus is leaning into the moment. Jesus here models the same three habits we have seen exhibited in witnessing communities: he expects God to move, recognizes when a special moment might be happening, and leans into that moment responsively.

THE THREE HABITS OF WITNESSING COMMUNITIES

The way witnessing communities view and respond to God's work around them differentiates them not only from huddled communities but also from other churches and communities that may be very evangelistically active (witness temperature seems really high) but who go about that evangelism in a quite different way. Some churches, for example, hold large annual evangelistic events that are very fruitful, but we would not really describe them as witnessing communities. Why not? Because they don't practice these three specific habits that seem to be at the core of witnessing communities.

1. Expect God moments. People in witnessing communities expect God to be at work around them. They expect his right hand to move. There is a community-wide, heartfelt sense that God is on the move and doing things all around them. This isn't just a charismatic church phenomenon but a deep, abiding belief that God is still alive, still active, still caring, still running after the lost sheep. It is a sense that God's Spirit is moving and that his right hand is still active. This expectancy is palpable in witnessing communities.

But it is an informed expectancy. These Christians have a biblically informed view of God's work. What makes God's heart beat? What do his actions in redemptive history lead us to expect him to be about even today? What interests God? In a witnessing community folks have answers to these questions. They have seen clearly in Scripture that God is actively interested in healing people, reconciling enemies, convicting the proud, and (most centrally) bringing people home again. He is interested in reconciling people to himself through the love and grace and sacrifice of Jesus. God is actively drawing people to his Son. As Jesus put it, "No one can come to me unless the Father who sent me draws him" (John 6:44 ESV).

Informed by the Scriptures, Christians in witnessing communities expect God to be drawing people around them to Jesus. This informed expectancy is a palpable worldview that colors how they view their lives and the people around them. I (Don) had a non-Christian neighbor in Boulder, Colorado, whom I was becoming close friends with but who seemed to have no interest at all in the gospel. This elderly woman was cynical, thoroughly secular, and quite anti-Christian. To be honest, I had pretty much given up hope that she would ever become a Christian. I didn't expect any God moments. But then I ran into the five thresholds and began to understand that there are little steps that people take toward Jesus, not just huge leaps. Informed by this understanding of how people come to faith, I found wonder and expectancy blossoming within my heart: *I wonder if God is moving in some small way in her life today? I wonder what her next step might be?* I found myself becoming more genuinely expectant and on the lookout for God moments with my neighbor.

This informed expectancy is found embedded in the culture of witnessing communities. People's eyes are wide open, expecting God to move, expecting God to draw people toward him step by step. This is so central in these communities that it becomes a sort of proactive expectancy. In other words, leaders have changed how they plan for worship services, program retreats, and train small group leaders *because* they expect God to move. They begin to proactively build in space for God moments. They not only create space in their schedules and worship services for God to work, but they also actively train their leaders in how to recognize and respond to God moments.

2. Recognize God moments. If God were to appear in a cloud or make someone glow or speak in a booming voice, it would be easy to recognize a God moment. But he rarely moves in such neon, extraordinary ways (even in the Bible). More often, God moves upon the landscape of people's hearts. This interior work is miraculous but can be subtle. (At the well, the disciples just saw the woman drop her bucket and run off. They didn't see everything that was going on in the tender places within her.) Even people who are becoming more expectant may need help and training in the habit of recognizing God moments.

In witnessing communities people are encouraged to look for God to be at work in all sorts of different places. Many Christians expect that God may be at work in a worship service or during a Bible study (these are God sorts of activities after all), but the Scriptures (and history) reveal that God is at work everywhere. Witnessing communities are on the lookout for God to be at work in their homes, neighborhoods, workplaces, schools, stores, games, etc.

Also, we need to be attentive for God to be at work on his own schedule. Jesus and the disciples were tired as they journeyed through Samaria. Perhaps the disciples were enjoying having a day off without being busy in ministry. Their expectation antennae were perhaps turned off. But Jesus was on the lookout. Years ago I (Don) was returning home from a trip to Chicago where I had taught several times and counseled hurting students. It was a jam-packed trip, and I practically collapsed into my seat on the airplane—thankful for all God had done and excited to unplug during the flight back home. To be honest, I was not expectant in that moment. I was tired. And yet when a simple exchange of pleasantries with the woman seated next to me caused her to start crying and processing deep pain in her life, I got the sense that maybe God was doing something right then, on his own schedule, in the appointed *kairos* moment.

Recognizing God moments means being attentive for little hints no matter where you are or when it is. Little hints—a quick tear, an earnest question, a heartfelt response, a real puzzling over something in the Bible, someone showing up that you didn't expect, a nudge from God to initiate—are meant to cause curiosity in the Christian: *I wonder if God is doing something here? Is this some kind of God moment? Is God's right hand being "valiant," as the psalmist celebrated?*

One feature of witnessing communities is that people often name God moments. This doesn't mean they speak out of turn and boldly proclaim, *God is doing something right now inside of you!* Such aggressive proclamations can be manipulative and, well, wrong. But there's something very different about giving voice to a potential God moment. Don, on that plane after a long conversation: *I wonder if maybe God wanted us to sit by each other because he's wanting you to resolve this issue in your life and find peace.* In a Bible study when a non-Christian is really stuck on a certain part: *It seems like there's something maybe God wants to say to you in this.* A worship leader who feels a nudge from God: *I'm wondering if maybe we should just linger here in this moment for a little bit. I think God may be doing something in the room right now.* These little ways of naming potential God moments are humble, exploratory, curious, wondering—and prayerful.

Naming potential God moments doesn't have to mean you are overly charismatic or presumptuous; it is simply a way of actively recognizing God moments. And it's a habit that we've noticed in witnessing communities of all sizes and types.

3. Respond to God moments. Folks in witnessing communities aren't just able to pick up on subtle clues and recognize God moments, but they also tend to be equipped and ready to respond to them. These responses don't have to be brilliant (responding in just the right way), but they do tend to be unhesitant (responding in the moment). While responses vary based on the specific situation and context, we've observed that in witnessing communities responses to God moments do tend to be humble, wise, and prayerful.

After preaching an Easter sermon titled "The Resurrection Files," I (Don) was approached by Anna, a young and thoughtful mother. I had seen Anna at services but did not know her well. With tears in her eyes, she said, "I need to experience what you just talked about. I need to be a Resurrection File." In the sermon I had told numerous stories of how people had come to Jesus and experienced inexplicable healing (emotional, physical, spiritual) because of the work of the resurrected Jesus in their lives. And here was this young woman who clearly needed some healing in her own life. The conviction in her voice, the tears in her eyes, the sense of the Holy Spirit with us as we talked—this was a God moment. She didn't just "like the sermon"; God's right hand was moving in the room, in her heart—and I recognized that this was the case.

But it didn't stop there. By God's grace I went on to respond to the God moment but in a simple, humble way. I didn't pretend to know this woman, to understand what kind of healing God wanted for her. So I responded immediately but tentatively. I named the moment: "It sounds like God is moving inside of you, that he has something for you, to give you." And then I brought Anna across the crowded room to where my wife, Wendy, was chatting with others. Wendy is a gifted spiritual director and prayer minister, and I figured that connecting Anna and Wendy was a good next step.

Responding to God moments by partnering with God, step by step along the way, is very different than presuming to know exactly what God is doing and taking over for him. God moments are just that—*God* moments. In witnessing communities folks respond right away to God moments, but they do so in a humble way.

Their responses also tend to be wise. This doesn't mean they are like gurus who always know the right thing to do—far from it. It means that folks in witnessing communities are often equipped with a fair amount of wisdom about how people tend to come to faith these days. This has been one of the fruits of the five thresholds: Christians have become more knowledgeable about how non-Christians journey toward Jesus. The five thresholds are a wisdom tool, a way of becoming familiar with the basic contours of the path toward Jesus. Having this wisdom tool allows us to respond to God moments with more wisdom. (See the introduction for an overview of the five thresholds.)

In church after church, community after community, we have seen the fruits that come from such wisdom. We've heard countless stories of people who confess that they usually had just one response to anyone they thought was a seeker, no matter where that seeker was on the journey. Intellectual types often went right to apologetic arguments, even if the person they were talking with was not asking questions. Prophetic types jumped right to an urgent call to convert, even if the person they were talking with didn't know them and in no way trusted them. Shy types tried to keep the conversation vague and exploratory, even if the person they were talking with was asking specific, heartfelt questions about the last couple issues they had to resolve before giving their life to Jesus.

One of our friends, Arthur, was helping lead a community out of their huddle. They prayed for God moments. They prayed for eyes to see where God was at work. And God was indeed at work, even helping a few new friends become followers of Jesus. But Arthur was skeptical, and so his response was skeptical: "That can't be a real conversion. I don't believe it." God was bringing a profound change in the community, but this influential member struggled to see the Holy Spirit bringing the God moments. Just like at UCSD, described in the introduction, there was a narrative at work in the huddled community, a story they believed about why evangelism did not work in their context. Arthur had a hard time letting go of that cynicism and responding wisely to what God was doing. And of course they struggled to celebrate the emerging faith of the new followers of Jesus. What is there to celebrate if these aren't sincere conversions? The good news is that after a year of being stuck in skepticism, Arthur's community did break the huddle. Now they are a witnessing community, they have a new narrative—that God can and will do more in their midst—and they are responsive to God moments. Today Arthur helps throw the parties each time there is a new follower of Jesus.

Just because we're responding to a God moment, it doesn't mean we are doing so in a wise way. In witnessing communities, folks seek after this wisdom. Folks become familiar with the path to faith and try to discern where their friends are on that journey. The reality is that non-Christians do not know how to journey toward Jesus or how to become Christians. They need friends and guides. They need folks who will respond to God moments with wisdom.

One year Don's wife, Wendy, was in a small group that happened to have a strong skeptic, Celeste, in attendance. Celeste was carrying lots of church-hurt around with her, but her curiosity about Jesus outweighed her distrust for Christians, so she had come to the group with a couple Christian friends. One night Celeste lingered after the meeting was done and began talking with Wendy about how the discussion that night had stoked within her a desire for the kind of healing she heard Jesus was capable of giving people. She urgently wanted healing inside.

Wendy recognized the God moment and asked Celeste if she could pray with her. "On one condition," Celeste replied. "I'll let you pray with me as long as you don't try to make me become a Christian." Not only did Wendy recognize that this woman was at the third threshold (opening up to change), but she wisely discerned that God's right hand was moving to bring healing to this woman. That was the Spirit's agenda that night. So Wendy responded, "I don't care if you become a Christian, Celeste. I want you to experience healing. And I think God wants that for you tonight." Wendy responded wisely to the God moment in front of her. It was *God's* moment, and Wendy entered into that moment where many of us might have been tempted to respond less wisely.

Now eventually Celeste did become a Christian, and she has become a great small group leader. Part of what makes her a good leader is that she herself is wise in how she responds to the God moments that happen during a small group. This is a fairly predictable feature in witnessing communities: people respond to God moments humbly and wisely. And they respond prayerfully.

In the midst of God moments, folks in witnessing communities aren't afraid to just "go live" and ask God what he is doing. Because God's right hand is active in the moment, it is a common practice for people to pause in the moment to ask God what he is doing. Many Christians can quote the beginning of Psalm 127:1, "Unless the LORD builds the house, those who build it labor in vain" (ESV). But not all of us think in the moment to ask, *God, what are you building here?* We've noticed this habit in witnessing communities: people respond prayerfully to God moments. This is perhaps why there tends to be a lack of stress or fear when a God moment arrives. While Christians in huddled communities tend to wilt or draw back in God moments (perhaps fearful of not knowing the exact way to respond), Christians in witnessing communities are generally not afraid of leaning into God moments. They not only expect God moments and recognize them, but they are also free to respond to them with humility, wisdom, and prayer.

THE REALITY AND HOPE OF BEING IN (AND EVEN LEADING) A WITNESSING COMMUNITY

If you've spent much time in a witnessing community, you've had the privilege of really getting what the psalmist was expressing in Psalm 118:15—glad songs of salvation are indeed in the tents of the righteous! Maybe we don't meet or live in tents anymore, but we still sing glad songs of salvation. It really is something to see God's right hand move in someone's life. It is thrilling and humbling and electric to see God draw someone to his Son, Jesus (see figure 2.2).

Witnessing communities have this in common as well: they sing glad songs. They tell and retell stories of how God has been changing people's lives. There's something about seeing multiple conversions every year that refreshes and exhilarates a community of believers. Leaders of witnessing communities are right to give space for these stories and songs and celebrations. This is one of the beautiful realities of leading a witnessing community.

Leaders of witnessing communities deal with a couple other realities that bear mentioning. First, they have to strive to keep mission at the center of their community. You'd think with all these "glad songs of salvation" that it would be easy to keep your evangelistic temperature warm, but that turns out not to be the case. If it is generally true that "vision leaks," then it is doubly true that vision for evangelism *really* leaks. A witnessing community left unattended will see their evangelistic temperature drop over time. A sort of spiritual entropy sets in, especially when it comes to evangelism (figure 2.3).

Witnessing Communities

Engaged in witness

- witness is a value
- some non-Christians are involved in community
- multiple conversions annually

Habits:

1. expect God moments
2. recognize God moments
3. respond to God moments

Figure 2.2. Habits of witnessing communities

While this is lamentable, it is reality. Leaders of witnessing communities need to keep the mission central to the community in word and deed. It's not enough to rely on past declarations of evangelistic emphasis. It's not enough to keep referring to past testimonies of conversion. We know one pastor who puts an "expiration date" of four months on any testimony. If it's older than four months, he won't use it as an example—he pushes himself for new testimonies all the time. By whatever means, leadership needs to act purposefully to keep the evangelism temperature of the community warm. All the tools of leadership (vision casting, modeling, programs, structures, storytelling, etc.) must be brought to bear to combat this natural evangelism entropy.

Huddled   **Witnessing**   **Conversion**

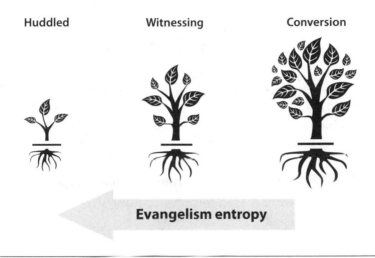

Evangelism entropy

Figure 2.3. Evangelism entropy

But why does evangelism vision tend to leak so quickly and persistently? The many human habits and temptations we looked at in the last chapter reveal a tendency within our own flesh toward being huddled. But beyond that, a very real enemy stands against Jesus' kingdom in very real ways. This is another reality of leading a witnessing community.

When a community begins to see their evangelism temperature increase they become more of a target for spiritual attack. Perhaps this is because when your community is huddled, it is relatively harmless to the enemy. The enemy is not interested in it. But once you start seeing the kingdom advance, the enemy is going to notice you. You will show up on his screen. So witnessing communities need to expect spiritual attack—in all its subtle and slimy forms.

Leaders of witnessing communities learn not to be surprised or blindsided by spiritual attack but to soberly face it and combat it.

While it would be a mistake to pay too much attention to the enemy (he doesn't deserve or warrant being at the center of our thinking or actions), it is also a mistake for leaders of witnessing communities to close their eyes to this reality. Leaders must be vigilant and exercise their leadership. Glad songs of salvation are not lullabies meant to lull a leader to blissful sleep; they are intended to bring glory to God and renewed energy to God's people.

Leaders of witnessing communities must be attentive to their own spiritual health and the spiritual health of their community. Not only do huddled temptations constantly pull at their flesh, but the enemy will try to distract believers with whispered lies and temptations. This is one of the reasons that the false dichotomy between evangelism and spiritual formation is so silly. A spiritually growing and mature body of believers will naturally find themselves caught up in God's work in this world. And a community that is active in God's work of evangelism will naturally face temptations and attack and need to constantly cling to Jesus.

The image Jesus suggested for his followers was that of branches: we abide in the vine and bear fruit. Is there a dichotomy between abiding and fruit bearing? The question is almost ludicrous. We are called to abide and bear fruit. In abiding in Jesus we receive life and joy and pruning. This causes us to bear fruit. In bearing fruit we face temptations and attack. This causes us to abide in Jesus all the more strongly. Leaders of witnessing communities need to meet this reality with care, keeping the evangelism temperature high while keeping the Jesus fire burning bright. We cling to Jesus and get caught up in his work. We labor in his work, which makes us cling ever more to him. This virtuous cycle is a beautiful thing to be a part of and see and is part of the hope of leading a witnessing community.

HOW DO YOU BREAK THE HUDDLE?

In part two we'll look in depth at how huddled communities can become witnessing communities, but for now here are some practices that can help us break the huddle and move toward becoming a witnessing community.

Practice prayer. Invite everyone in your huddle to begin praying daily for the people around them who are not yet Jesus followers. (We like to use a prayer map for this purpose, like you saw at the end of chapter one.)

Root your vision in Scripture. Brainstorm with your huddle their favorite passages about witness, evangelism, or conversion. Cast vision for what your huddle can become using one or more of these core passages.

Practice breaking the huddle. Change how you end all of your meetings and gatherings. Before your closing prayer or benediction, remind everyone why you have been huddled and why you now break and go out to the playing field for the rest of life. We gather in order to go, bless, love, serve, and show Christ to our friends and neighbors and our hurting world.

Witnessing communities may be a bit messy to lead (things are live and real and relational), but there is a joy to all this mess. Being attentive to God moments can take away from our sense of control (*Can't God move when it works well in my schedule?*), but there is unmistakable life. This is the hope of leading a witnessing community: being a part of the church as it was meant to be, in all its mess and beauty and purpose and victory. For those who have seen a community move from being huddled to witnessing there is a great sense of joy—the contrast between the two is almost indescribable. To go from no conversions to multiple conversions a year? To go from the tunnel vision of huddled concerns to the horizon vision of kingdom expansion? To trade in decent program moments to surprising God moments? When that evangelism temperature climbs, there is life and joy and laughter and amazement and tears and struggle. It is a beautiful thing to be a part of.

PRAYER

Father, please give us more of yourself, more of your Son, Jesus, and more of your Spirit. James 1:5 says that if we lack wisdom, we should ask you and you will give wisdom without reproach. I want more wisdom about how to lean into the God moments around me. I believe you are more at work in me and around me than I can see today. Open my eyes. Help me to be bold yet sensitive as my friends have God moments. I pray that for my community as well. We long to see more people transformed. Please increase our evangelism temperature. Take our old narratives and skepticism. Please move your mission more powerfully to the center of who we are. And protect us from the evil one as we move forward in the powerful name of Jesus. Amen.

DISCUSSION

1. Which of the three habits of witnessing communities do we practice the most? Give examples.

    • expecting God moments

    • recognizing God moments

    • responding to God moments

2. Which of these three habits of witnessing communities do we practice the least? Why?

3. Name three non-Christian friends you want to pray for.

3

CONVERSION COMMUNITIES

Aligned Around Witness

It is a beautiful thing to behold when a community moves from being huddled to witnessing. The joy of a God moment is contagious, and there is nothing that reinvigorates believers like seeing someone journey through the five thresholds and come to faith in Jesus. When a once-huddled community grows and stretches and becomes involved in witness, we believe there is rejoicing in heaven, just as there is here on earth.

But for some witnessing community leaders the joy is paired with a nagging sense of discontent. Multiple conversions a year is wonderful . . . but what if you used to see multiple conversions *per month*? God moments are incredible . . . but what if you've seen robust God *movements* in the past where many people were caught up in something God was doing?

During an interview, Matthew Hemsley, then associate rector at Truro, asked me (Don) more about the three types of communities we were exploring in this book. When I described them, Matt grew quiet and thoughtful. He asked several follow-up questions about the third type, a conversion community. Matthew then told me about the church in London where he became a

Christian—St. Paul's, Onslow Square—which he now understood was a conversion community. The church was aligned around witness. Numerous non-Christians were involved in the life of the church, and they saw multiple adult conversions every month.

Our discussion had given Matthew language to fully understand and describe the difference between Truro (a witnessing community) and what he had experienced as a new believer at St. Paul's, Onslow Square (a conversion community). And this clear distinction brought with it a holy sense of discontent within Matthew. *Is there more our church right now could be experiencing? Is there something I could be doing differently as a leader to help this evangelistic community grow?* This is a holy kind of hope and wondering. Even as I was interviewing him about his community, we had a God moment. God was inviting Matthew into more: more of the power of his Spirit, more of the harvest, more joy. He was stoking the holy discontent within Matthew.

This is part of the hope of leading a witnessing community: God just might be preparing that community for the next step of their growth. God might be calling that community to raise its temperature and become a conversion community (figure 3.1).

Huddled	Witnessing	Conversion

Limited witness	*Engaged in witness*	*Aligned around witness*
• witness is a concept	• witness is a value	• witness shapes everything
• non-Christian presence in community is rare	• some non-Christians are involved in community	• many non-Christians involved in community
• conversions are rare	• multiple conversions annually	• multiple conversions monthly

Figure 3.1. Three stages of witnessing communities

CONVERSION COMMUNITIES

As we saw in chapter two, a witnessing community is one where God moments are expected, recognized, and responded to. God seems to be drawing a friend of ours to him, so we respond by partnering with him as he journeys along the five thresholds. When these journeys culminate with a friend's decision to become a Christian, we've got a wonderful God moment on our hands. That's when a witnessing community celebrates what God has done. *There is a new believer in our midst!* In many communities that God moment creates a warm glow that radiates for some time.

While such God moments and the inspiration they provide are wonderful, God-breathed miracles, we have found that in the kingdom of God they don't have to be the end of the story. Some Christian communities see every God moment not just as the climax of a wonderful story but as the introduction to a much larger story. Some communities see every God moment as the potential beginning to a God *movement* that might involve many more people.

What exactly does it mean for a God moment to become a God movement? Consider my (Doug's) friend Eddie and his God moment. On a hilltop at a retreat, Eddie decided to give his life to Jesus. It was quite a God moment! (I'll tell you more about that retreat and Eddie's story in chapter five.) But now I want to draw your attention to what happened *next*—Eddie's God moment became a God movement.

About ten of us were gathered with Eddie on that hilltop, and we witnessed firsthand God embracing Eddie. Now this is when something very interesting happened. Instead of assuming that God's work was done for the day and going back down the mountain to celebrate what God had done, we lingered there on the top of the hill. We didn't rush on from the God moment but sat in it and looked around to see what else God might be up to. When we finished praying for Eddie, my coleader, John, asked the other seekers gathered there: "Who else would like to experience the love of God and come home to your heavenly Father?" (This is a common feature in conversion communities: lingering in a God moment to see who else God might be working in. On that day it turned out God was nowhere near done working!)

After John's invitation, Oscar stepped forward, quivering. I distinctly remember how Oscar walked over and stood on the exact spot where Eddie had stood and cried just moments before. Oscar put his hands out in an open posture of receiving from God, exactly like Eddie had. And he tilted his head downward, just like Eddie had. As we prayed for Oscar, he began to tremble and cry as he experienced the power of the Holy Spirit embracing him. The single God moment was actually turning into a God movement! We then invited the other seekers there on the hilltop to consider this step of faith. By God's grace, by the end of the retreat, eight of the fifteen seekers had become followers of Jesus. The God moment did not end with Eddie. In fact, his risky step of public faith built momentum and became the doorway, the trigger, the spark that began a mini–conversion movement within our little community. God used Eddie's decision to move his peers through the thresholds more quickly. The ability to follow Jesus for themselves (threshold #5) became more real, tangible, attractive, and inspiring.

In conversion communities people making decisions to follow Jesus becomes the new normal. A conversion isn't a rare sight to behold but a common sight—at times such decisions seem to happen weekly. These communities have a great faith and confidence in God that he can do more than we currently see. Leaders respond nimbly to whatever God is doing, and they are willing to adjust structures and schedules accordingly. The members sense that we hear the word from God, and we respond in any way that God might be leading. These communities are joyful and thriving, not complacent. We call these conversion communities because they are indeed marked by regular conversions.

Some conversion communities have a dramatic story of culture change that was inspired by a movement of prayer, leading to a large number of faith decisions in a short amount of time. This conversion momentum changes the community from the inside out and sets them on a path to seek God for more.

Others become conversion communities through small steps of faith in the same direction over many years. They have been faithfully and prayerfully changing every part of their ministry structures to create space for non-Christians to engage and make decisions to follow Jesus. The leaders of these communities are trained to help someone make a faith decision as the most critical part of their leadership training.

Some conversion communities are thriving within one specific ethnic group. We know of a Spanish-speaking Latino church in the LA area that sees about three hundred conversions per year and their overall church size is under a thousand. They invite extended family members to come to the Sunday service, where there are invitations to faith, and God is releasing movements of his Spirit through family networks.

Other conversion communities are some of the famous and celebrated megachurches. Their leadership works hard to pray, to keep casting vision, to offer training, to create dynamic events that together God uses to stoke the fire of evangelistic passion and fruit. It is not easy for these large conversion communities to maintain their conversion fruit, but their leadership teams toil day in and day out to do just that.

Though conversion communities can look quite different from each other, they all seem to have a number of features in common:

- They have an explicit vision to love and serve more people with the gospel this year than last year.

- They know how to help a God moment become a God movement.

- The community hears many testimonies of new believers.

- Members have ongoing opportunities to receive training, encouragement, and motivation to be witnesses.

- Structures, programs, and up-front leadership are shaped around the assumption that some folks in the room might be ready to make a decision of faith.

- The number of folks coming to faith each year is more than 10 percent of the adult attendance.

What happened on that hilltop with Eddie and the others was incredible. But it wasn't extraordinary. It turns out that this phenomenon (God moments turning into God movements) is actually a built-in feature of God's kingdom. Just consider what happened after that incredible God moment between Jesus and the woman at the well.

JOHN 4: THE WOMAN AT THE WELL AND HER VILLAGE

Picking up where we left off, the woman is so excited about finding living water that she leaves behind her water jar. The sole reason she came to the well in the first place is long forgotten as she returns to her village and tells them, "Come, see a man who told me all that I ever did. Can this be the Christ?" (John 4:29 ESV). The very woman who gets water at midday to hide from her community the shame she feels about her five husbands uses this same information to help her village get to know the man who changed her life.

It turns out this simple, authentic testimony of faith from the woman is enough to pique the village's curiosity about Jesus. Her vulnerable testimony seems to engender trust (threshold #1) and arouse curiosity about Jesus (threshold #2). As John relates what happens, we understand her testimony as the bridge between the God moment at the well and the God movement in her village. Their journey toward Jesus begins when they hear her story and continues once they meet Jesus for themselves.

This is a core assumption at play in conversion communities: the joy at seeing a God moment is paired with the clear expectation that any God moment might be the start of a God movement. This seems to be the assumption that Jesus has. Though the woman at the well has fled, Jesus does not assume the story is over. Jesus lingers at the well. He expects that after the moment there may come a movement. He expects that she will share her story of freedom with the rest of her village. He expects that the impact of her story could lead to a movement in the village. John narrates the dynamic/ironic scene with Jesus and his disciples perfectly. While the disciples are mostly confused about why Jesus would speak to this woman and wondering whether he has eaten food, Jesus knows that this God moment at the well is leading to something more. The whole village is so curious about Jesus that they are coming out to the well en masse. "They went out of the town and were coming to him" (John 4:30 ESV).

Jesus doesn't want the disciples to miss what is happening or how his kingdom works, so he interprets for them just what *has* happened (the God moment) and what is *about to happen* (the God movement). "Jesus said to them, 'My food is to do the will of him who sent me and to accomplish his work. Do you not say, "There are yet four months, then comes the harvest"? Look, I tell you, lift up your eyes, and see that the fields are white for harvest'" (John 4:34-35 ESV). While the disciples are looking down at their current situation (they are mostly concerned about whether Jesus has eaten recently), Jesus is inviting them to lift up their eyes and see the fields that are ripe for harvest. "Look!" he says, and as he says this a spiritual harvest is literally walking toward them from the village. John makes it very clear: Jesus wanted the disciples not only to linger in the God moment of what happened to the woman but, like him, to lift up their eyes to see what else God might be doing.

Finally, Jesus is clear that he wants the disciples to labor in that harvest with him.

> Already the one who reaps is receiving wages and gathering fruit for eternal life, so that sower and reaper may rejoice together. For here the saying holds true, "One sows and another reaps." I sent you to reap that for which you did not labor. Others have labored, and you have entered into their labor. (John 4:36-38 ESV)

Jesus is inviting the disciples to get ready to interact with this crowd from the village, to labor. It's harvest time and he expects them to labor alongside him in reaping the beautiful fruits of that harvest.

Notice that he is clear that they haven't caused the harvest. They are entering into someone else's labor—God's. Jesus wants them to be crystal clear that this is a God movement, not a disciple movement.

This part of the story in John 4 is gorgeous and powerful and moving. The good news is that we have seen this same dynamic lived out again and again in conversion communities in our own day. God moments still spark God movements. There are communities where single conversions actually lead to other conversions— a real harvest. There are communities where the image of harvest isn't just an inspiring metaphor but an accurate descriptor of what is happening on an ongoing basis. After living in and meeting with many of these conversion communities, we've noticed some simple but profound habits that are at play in them. Understanding these habits can help us discern how to help our own community take steps toward becoming a conversion community.

THE THREE HABITS OF CONVERSION COMMUNITIES

For starters, every conversion community we've been a part of has the same habits as the witnessing communities that we looked at in chapter three (they expect God moments, recognize God moments, and respond to God moments). But in addition to that, they also exhibit these three habits. Conversion communities

1. linger in God moments,

2. lift up their eyes, and

3. labor in the harvest.

It has been striking to notice how these three habits are present in the leadership and membership of various conversion communities. While it would be overstating matters to suggest that doing these three things will automatically create mass conversions (after all, these are *God* movements we're talking about), it is meaningful that Jesus' actions in John 4 (and his encouragement to his disciples) seems to have a lot in common with the habits that are active in conversion communities today. It's worth our time to consider these three habits in detail.

Conversion communities linger in God moments. Just as Jesus lingered at the well near this woman's Samaritan village after her incredible God moment, so folks in conversion communities seem to have the habit of not rushing on from a great work of God.

Think back to that hilltop after Eddie became a Christian. How many of us would have been tempted to give Eddie a huge hug, cry in amazement, and rush back down to camp to tell others just what had happened? This is actually a quite reasonable response. But leaders in conversion communities have either been trained (or have the instincts) not to rush away so quickly. Instead of rushing off to write a prayer letter about the great and marvelous God moment that happened (*Eddie became a Christian! We had an actual conversion at camp!*), folks in conversion communities simply linger in the moment. They are attentive to God in the moment.

Jesus didn't hike out of Samaria after God cut to the heart of this desperate woman. He stayed in Samaria, attentive to what else God might be doing. Waiting to see what would happen, John and Doug didn't rush everyone back down from the hilltop. They lingered in the moment, attentive to what else God might want to do.

Or consider Peter in Acts 2. What happened at Pentecost was one of the greatest God moments of all time. God's Spirit was poured out on his church. This moment was incredible—tongues of fire, foreign languages being spoken, the presence of God in their midst, God's Spirit "making his home" inside their hearts. On some level this had to be an overwhelming experience for the disciples. Think of what this would have been like for Peter, the leader of the group. Anyone who has ever led a group in the midst of a God moment knows what a unique challenge it is to lead and shepherd a people in the midst of God doing something extraordinary and new.

Of course Peter had watched Jesus lead in similar situations, responding to God moments in the midst of chaos. Think of the demoniac (a crazed naked man running straight at Jesus), the bleeding woman (crowds pressing in on Jesus from all sides), and Jairus's daughter being raised from the dead (the cynical crowds, the loud wails of the hired mourners), to name three. And that was all on the same day! (Check out Mark 5.) Perhaps the noise in Jerusalem, the messy frenzy in the crowd, and the confusion of conflicting reports about what was happening there on Pentecost were vaguely familiar to Peter!

We do know that Peter saw the God moment in the chaos. Peter lingers there in the God moment: he doesn't rush off to figure out alone what was going on, he doesn't take off with the disciples to celebrate this miraculous outpouring, he doesn't hide from the crowds that are forming. Peter lingers. He pays attention. He remains attentive to what God might be doing. This same habit is present in conversion communities today: they see God moments not as a wonderful end but as a potential beginning of something else. As for Peter, he lingers at Pentecost and ultimately gets to participate in God unleashing the mother of all God movements.

One thing that has helped us linger in God moments is changing how we pray. We practice listening prayer both individually and in our communities. We ask, "Lord, what are you trying to say to us?" Our friend James Choung has learned to linger in God moments. Recently he was speaking at UCLA from John 1. His talk was aimed at skeptics. He told the story of Nathaniel, who believed in Jesus merely because Jesus told him that he saw him under a fig tree. James said that is a "pretty dumb reason" to believe. And that became a repeated refrain. He ended his talk with a disarming question: "What is something dumb that Jesus could show you to help you believe in him?" James used the Ignatian colloquy approach to pray for the skeptics in the room that night:

- Let's have a quiet moment. We are going to listen to Jesus and see if he has something to say to you personally.

- Picture yourself sitting on a stool in a darkish room. How do you feel?

- There is a door in front of you. Jesus walks into the room. What is he wearing?

- Jesus looks you straight in the eye. He greets you. What does he say to you?
- Then he tells you he loves you. He leans in to whisper something in your ear. He tells you something that he has been wanting to tell you for a long time. What does he tell you?
- Now tell your neighbor what Jesus said to you.
- Now I invite you to act on what you heard.

Gabby happened to be visiting the group that evening. During the listening prayer, she heard Jesus say to her, "Follow me." So Gabby decided to respond to that invitation, and she did exactly what Jesus prompted; she became a follower of Jesus.

Listening prayer allows us to dream—what if the times when we feel God's presence are the beginning of a movement. *Lord, give us a picture of what this person or community might be like in a year. Lord, how might you use this struggle we are facing right now for some kingdom purpose?*

Folks in conversion communities are in the habit of lingering in God moments. The good news is, this is not a tricky habit to develop. Any of us who are fortunate enough to experience a God moment can learn to slow down and linger in the moment, developing the hope and faith and active expectation in such moments to be attentive to God, not only by thanking him for what he's done but by asking him what else he might be up to.

The truth is, it can be exhausting (and exhilarating) to be part of a God moment, and there's a temptation to take a break after a great moment. There is a kind of letdown. *Boy, I spent a lot of time walking with my friend during her journey. And now we've arrived! We've crossed the finish line! I'm think I'm going to go take a nap . . .* But folks in conversion communities don't lean back after a God moment, they lean forward: expectant, curious, prayerful, attentive to God. They also become very attentive to the people around them.

Conversion communities lift up their eyes. Just as Jesus lifted up his eyes to see the harvest that was ripe (and encouraged the disciples to do the same), so folks in conversion communities seem to have the habit of lifting up their eyes to look around them in the midst of God moments. Jesus' command to his disciples (who seemed to be caught up in other concerns) was very simple: *Look! Look around you at the fields that are ripe for harvest. Look up from your petty concerns about lingering in Samaria and see the people all around you.*

This may seem like a simple habit, but it is not easy. Recall that the disciples did not like Samaritans. They had been trained their whole lives to consider Samaria the land of unfaithfulness and uncleanness. God was not pleased with the Samaritans, right? They were shocked to find Jesus talking with a Samaritan woman. So Jesus had to command them to look at the Samaritans who were walking toward them from the village and to see them not as outcasts or half-breeds or unclean people but as a harvest. Harvests are good! Harvests are beautiful! A harvest is something God does! And Jesus wants the disciples to follow his own lead: not settling for a wonderful encounter with this woman but looking around to see who else God might want to get caught up in what is going on.

Let's go back to that hilltop with Doug. One of the mysterious things about communities is how they grow together. One member tries something, and the others watch and are inspired and want to try it also. We learn together. We practice faith together. That was happening through the retreat in our little community. It is a beautiful thing to watch and enjoy together. Little steps of risk and honesty become contagious, the new normal in that community. Eddie's public moment of transparency and vulnerability helped us all believe God for more. His amazing interaction with God felt like we were in that moment with God. It was not just for Eddie. We were being changed by it as well.

I (Doug) and my coleader, John, decided to linger in the God moment. Actually, John and I had privately prayed that morning that the hike would be just like we saw it unfolding. Even though I had never been in a moment like that before, we had hoped for it. That allowed us to lift up our eyes and look around. Who else is here? Who else might God be moving in? Could Eddie's God moment actually be the spark of a God movement? Asking this question ("Who else would like to experience the love of God and come home to your heavenly Father?") seemed to slow down time for us and allowed us to look around at their faces. Such questions are an important part of this habit. And it turned out God was doing more that day. There was a ripe harvest right in our midst. This Jesus-commanded habit of lifting up our eyes to look for the harvest seems to be a key feature in the leadership and membership of conversion communities.

Again, consider Peter at the beginning of Acts. Not only does he linger in this wonderful Pentecost God moment, he lifts his eyes up to look around him. Where some of us might have been tempted to focus on ourselves (*Wow, what is God doing in me right now?*) or our own flock (*Okay, is anyone freaking out right now about all these foreign languages?*), Peter lifts his eyes to consider the harvest all around him. There's a large crowd forming in Jerusalem. Recall that the last time this happened Peter wound up running for his life because the crowds were out to get Jesus! He and the other disciples had been staying in locked rooms for fear of the crowds in Jerusalem. No one would have blamed Peter for ducking his head in the midst of this growing crowd and shepherding the disciples back to their room.

Instead Peter not only lingers in the God moment, but he then lifts his eyes up. He looks around at the crowds. And what crowds they were! God's timing was excellent: he sent his Spirit right in the middle of Pentecost. God had brought "all nations" right to their doorstep since Jews and God-fearers had journeyed from everywhere to be in Jerusalem for the feast. And Peter looks at these crowds and sees a potential harvest. "But Peter, standing with the eleven, lifted up his voice and addressed them: 'Men of Judea and all who dwell in Jerusalem, let this be known to you, and give ear to my words'" (Acts 2:14 ESV).

One shift that helps us lift up our eyes is changing how we look at people. This is essentially what Jesus was saying to the disciples. Change how you look at this woman. Change how you look at this village. Sometimes we look at people and only see that they showed up at our worship service. But do we notice when someone who is normally quiet starts to become more vocal? When someone who is normally low-key expresses passion? Do we notice gifts that are less obvious—those who go out of their way to welcome people, those who listen to people a little bit more? Do we notice when someone stays late? Do we notice the signs when people are wanting to talk?

Our friend Dan was in the middle of a bad leadership team meeting—bad because it was boring and no one seemed excited to be there. Dan remembered a previous great interaction with Tom, when Tom had told him a story about a group of people that God put on his heart. He had been praying for them daily. Tom was also part of this boring meeting. So Dan took a risk. He changed the subject and put Tom on the spot. "Tom, tell us about the people God has put on your heart to pray for." As he shared, other people's faces lit up. They got excited about Tom's growing love and burden. It transformed their meeting. They could now feel the hope that God might want to reach that group of people, and everyone there could see that Tom was being empowered by God to do it. Dan said, "Tom, I think God is speaking to you as he is increasing your love and burden for this group of people. And I think God is speaking *through* you to all of us as well. How can we all we lean into this?" Dan led the group in a moment of listening prayer. "Jesus, what would you like to say to us about this? We are open to your leading." The next day, they had a follow-up conversation with Tom. They set him free from his current leadership responsibilities and blessed him to chase this new ministry vision. In hindsight, this was a turning point in their witnessing community becoming a conversion community. Thank God that Dan lifted up his eyes and paid attention to God's work in an unassuming person!

Another friend, Ryan, was part of a team doing in-depth listening prayer with a woman who was struggling with an eating disorder. It was a powerful prayer time, and clearly God was doing something. Instead of handing her a tissue and giving her a goodbye hug, Ryan lingered. He felt inspired to cast vision for how God might transform her brokenness. He declared, "A year from now, you will share this story of your struggle with others, and your story will become good news for other women with the same struggle." She began to cry tears of hope. This had never occurred to her before. Her disorder had made her feel disqualified from laboring in the harvest. Ryan's faith that God could minister through her weakness triggered new faith and vision within her. Thank God that Ryan lifted up his eyes!

Folks in conversion communities are in the habit of lifting their eyes up to look at the people around them. The good news is that anyone can develop this habit. Granted, there is much in our flesh and overall inertia that would keep us from initiating with a wide circle of folks in the wake of a God moment. But it is very possible to develop eyes to notice the people around us and to ask, Who might get caught up in the movement caused by this wonderful moment?

Conversion communities labor in the harvest. Just as Jesus invited his disciples to enter into the labor of the harvest, so folks in conversion communities see themselves as laborers on a very exciting kingdom farm. Anyone who has ever worked on a farm knows that when the harvest is ripe, all other agendas take a back seat. There will be plenty of time for fence-painting and sock-darning and engine-tuning after the harvest, but while the fields are ripe for harvest, the laborers of the farm are on the move. This is exactly the kind of natural urgency Jesus was conveying to his disciples there in Samaria: they were concerned about whether Jesus had eaten dinner. Jesus was concerned about something else: doing the will of the Father. When the harvest is ripe, it's time for God's people to enter into the labors with all they have.

When John and I (Doug) sensed back on that hilltop that there was a God movement afoot, we didn't hesitate and we didn't relax. We entered into the labor. This labor can be varied: inviting people to take a step forward in their faith, talking with people, praying with others, praying for others—whatever the harvest requires.

Think of how Peter on Pentecost enters into the labor of the harvest. First, he helps the folks around him understand what is going on. Some are curious. Some are confused. Some are skeptical, offering their cynical interpretation of what is happening: *the disciples are drunk!* Folks there were around threshold #2, curious about what was going on. So Peter enters into the labor and wisely addresses their question, opening their eyes to a completely different way of seeing the situation. He quotes from their own Scriptures and gives a fantastic redemptive-historical overview of the larger story Jesus and they are a part of. He explains what's going on.

Toward the end of his speech, Peter boldly goes right after their culpability, culminating with the cutting, "You killed him." He helps them see how their story is intertwined with the Jesus story. And the result is that the Spirit convicts them. "Now when they heard this they were cut to the heart" (Acts 2:37 ESV). They listen and engage. Their hearts are softened, convicted by what they've heard. They are open to this message (reminiscent of threshold #3). Peter pauses and waits for them to respond. Now they are clearly seekers. "What shall we do?" they ask. They want help taking a next step. And Peter helps them through threshold #5 en masse!

We have adopted a few important habits that help us learn to labor in the harvest. For example, we have changed how we help new believers. When someone makes a decision to follow Jesus we help them tell their story of faith to their friends over the next couple weeks. We coach them so that they can best describe what their life was like before the decision, what helped them make the decision to follow, and what has happened since the decision. We help them pray and invite their friends to an event where they can share their testimonies. After they share, we do another invitation to faith or invite their friends to be part of a small group. We try to intentionally pay attention to the "village behind every woman at the well" and see how God might be wooing the whole village.

Consider Mary's story. Mary was helping to lead an outreach on campus in response to studying John 4 with her community. In the same way that Jesus was uncovering the woman's thirst, the idea was to help students think about what they are thirsty for. The team got T-shirts with a red solo cup graphic and the simple word "Thirsty?" Before the outreach, Mary was hanging out in the dorm and met Angelica. They struck up a conversation. Angelica seemed eager, open, and responsive. Even though Mary had a hunch that Angelica was not yet a follower of Jesus, she said, "I'm doing this cool thing tomorrow called 'Thirsty?' Want to do it with me?" Angelica jumped at the chance.

Angelica was a great conversationalist during the outreach, especially when it came to asking people, "What do you think Jesus means when he says he has living water to offer us?" A few days later, Angelica came to the worship service and Bible study. At the end, the speaker explained what it means to embrace Jesus' living water for yourself and become his follower. Angelica was the first to respond. The penny dropped for her. What she had been offering to other people, Jesus' living water, she now embraced for herself!

In the past, we would have insisted that Angelica become a follower of Jesus herself first before helping lead an outreach with us. But Jesus has taught us that sometimes he moves much more quickly and in reverse order from our tidy plan. Laboring in the harvest means that we try to help develop anyone that God puts around us. The disciples see a Samaritan woman, but Jesus sees a potential witness being raised up.

THE REALITY AND HOPE OF BEING IN (AND EVEN LEADING) A CONVERSION COMMUNITY

What an incredible day for the kingdom Pentecost was. And what an incredible day for Peter. He learns what it is like to see a God moment (the disciples receiving the Holy Spirit) turn into a God movement (three thousand people repent and are baptized). On that day, the disciples learn what it is like to be a part of a God movement, and Peter takes steps toward becoming a movement leader. He learns to linger in God moments, he learns to lift his eyes up to see the people around him, and he learns the joy (the sometimes exhausting, incredible, life-changing joy) of entering into the labor of the harvest. He learns that sometimes urgency is the best pastoral approach.

This pattern of movement leadership repeats itself throughout Acts, throughout church history and even today in conversion communities throughout the world. Movement leadership is a hope-filled way to live your life, always looking for where God is at work, expecting to be invited into the process with God. It is actually possible for us to develop and grow as movement leaders.

Conversion Communities

Aligned around witness

- witness shapes everything
- many non-Christians involved in community
- multiple conversions monthly

Habits:

1. linger in God moments
2. lift up eyes on the fields
3. labor in the harvest

Figure 3.2. Habits of conversion communities

John and Doug's leadership with Eddie and that group on the hill is a great example. John led in some very specific ways that helped facilitate a moment turning into a movement. We expected that Eddie's decision, his moment, might pave the way for a small movement of conversion. In fact, we brought the group on the hike with just this hope and prayer. We could have had a private conversation with Eddie and with each member individually. But by inviting that group of non-Christians together to consider following Jesus, we expected and created space in case God wanted to tip the momentum into a community-wide conversion movement.

John expects God to work. And once God works, he is not satisfied. He could have just left it as Eddie's moment. In the past, we have done that many times. A conversion is celebrated, and no one asks, "What else might God be doing here? Might there be a movement being unleashed?" But John had been learning to be a movement leader. So John leaned in. "Who else wants to experience God in this way?" It's a simple, non-threatening invitation. It is neither manipulative nor inappropriate. By asking this question, he created space. He expected more, and he got to see God do more and more.

We can all grow in our leadership—even movement leadership. John has himself become an anointed and fruitful movement leader today. At the time of publishing, John Teter serves as the head of church planting for the Evangelical Covenant denomination. God is using him to plant and grow witnessing communities all over the country and world. He still expects God to show up, he still leans into God moments, and he still expects God to do more and more. By the way, John and I (Doug) are still monthly prayer partners fifteen years after this story. Eddie is John's very good friend today and a powerful leader in his cross-cultural, socially diverse, Acts 2 type of church. The movement continues!

To be honest, being involved in God movements can be confusing, risky, and messy. However, it is life-changing—and not just for the leader. The God movement at Pentecost strengthens the believers, and a new culture of amazing generosity and faith and joy is formed. The harvest inspires the laborers, which in turn emboldens their witness, and conversions become the new normal. Day by day new believers are added. That's what conversion communities are like. God's Spirit continues the great momentum in them and through them. Because of this first conversion community our world will never be the same.

And we have had the honor of seeing this pattern repeated again and again, though on much smaller scales. We are convinced that God wants and intends for his God moments to spark God movements. We have seen that witnessing communities can take steps toward becoming conversion communities by lingering in God moments, lifting up their eyes, and entering into the labor.

Does this mean that we, as Christian leaders, can create God movements on our own? Absolutely not. Just as we are powerless to create a single God moment, we are powerless to create a God movement. God is the one at work. But he is also calling his people into that work with him. Just as Jesus invited his disciples to enter into the God moment with the Samaritan woman and then into the God movement of her village, so God invites us to partner with him even today. These three habits are ways that we've seen Christians faithfully respond to that invitation.

Does this mean that if you develop these habits you will automatically see multiple conversions in your community every month? Nope. There is mystery involved here. No one can come to Jesus unless the Father draws them. In conversion communities people expect that God is calling people to himself and are taking steps to be a part of that work as it unfolds. Leaders in conversion communities are learning how to faithfully shepherd their communities to be attentive and responsive to the work that God is about. Just as Jesus invited his food-focused disciples to lift up their eyes and see the harvest, so today leaders can help their communities develop these same habits.

We understand that this may sound pretty simplistic. Three habits? The good news is that once you become comfortable with God movements, it really can be that straightforward. However, it is not easy. To embrace God movements is to be stretched in all kinds of ways. God invites us into new ways of believing, responding, and letting go of control. We become flexible. Nimble. Learners. Adaptive. Risk takers. Willing to be very uncomfortable.

We believe that God can transform witnessing communities into conversion communities where people making new faith decisions in Jesus becomes the norm. In all of this process, leadership matters. Whether you are part of a huddled community, a witnessing community, or a conversion community, there are steps you can take to grow yourself as a witness and to help inspire your community to grow its witness.

PRAYER

Father, you are amazing in how you see people and how you see villages. Please help me to see people and communities like you do. When I see you at work, remind me to lift up my eyes and ask you, "What else might you be doing here?" Help me to expect more. Please help me to relinquish my grasp on my agenda and my plan for the day. Make me more responsive to you. Take our fears. Give us a spirit of courage.

[Listening Prayer] Lord, in this quiet space, would you right now bring to mind one person in whom you are at work? One person to whom you are inviting me to reach out in love? Amen.

DISCUSSION

1. Which of the three habits of conversion communities do we practice the most? Which do we practice the least? Please describe.

   • lingering in God moments

   • lifting up our eyes

   • laboring in the harvest

2. How might we be like the woman with the eating disorder? How might God take an area of your personal pain or brokenness and use it to bring good news to others a year from now?

3. How might we be like Tom, the guy with a heart to reach a new group of people? Who is on your heart to pray for and reach out to in love?

4. If I could invite my non-Christian friends to attend one event in our community, which would I pick? Why? What would make this event even more attractive to my friends?

5. Who in our community is passionate about seeing their non-Christian friends know Jesus? How can I encourage them?

PART TWO

TWO MACRO-STRATEGIES FOR BREAKING THE HUDDLE

Huddled   Witnessing   Conversion

Nurture discipleship momentum

Embrace God movements

Mobilize relational evangelism

Align vision, structures, and people

4

NURTURE DISCIPLESHIP MOMENTUM

I (Val) remember hearing about the conversion community at UCSD and feeling a jumble of emotions. I felt inspired and thought, *Wow, that is the kind of community I want to join. Sign me up!* I felt curious. *How on earth did this happen? How did they so profoundly transform the culture of their community?* I asked a lot of questions. I wanted to understand the intricacies of what they were doing and how they were doing it. But to be very honest, I was skeptical. *It can't be that good. They must be making this up or exaggerating the fruit.* And sadly, I was just plain jealous and insecure. *What is wrong with me that I can't do this? I wish this were my story.* Then I felt guilty for feeling jealous because we all know jealousy is a sin!

Instead of celebrating and thanking God for his work at UCSD, I was focused on me. I tried to lean into my curious feelings, but first I had to acknowledge there were darker feelings lurking around and invite God into them. I am very grateful to say that God used this season of darker feelings to transform me. I certainly would not be part of this writing trio if I had not invited God into my insecurity and envy. After working this through with God, I became an avid learner, and I interviewed those connected with the amazing story. As I listened carefully, I tried to mimic their every step, anxiously seeking to get it right. It would have been wiser for me to ask God, "What are you saying to me through this? What are you inviting me to consider?"

If you are having any of these darker feelings, try to identify them. God is not surprised by the mixed emotions in our hearts and souls. He longs to be with you and give you hope. And please keep reading. This book is not for expert consultants on how to bring change to huddled communities. This book is for people who are open to the Holy Spirit and want to learn how he brings transformation to individuals and communities.

As you may know, great sports teams win championships with excellent fundamentals. Smart coaches do not allow their players to get sloppy and outgrow good fundamentals. This next section is getting into the fundamentals of wonderful witnessing communities. This shift in writing style will make sense to those of you who are motivated by the nuts and bolts. Others may prefer the visionary stories, the big picture, and the values in the first three chapters. Please don't put down the book when we shift gears a little. The fundamentals are the backbone of communities like UCSD. Their hard work with the basics, plus reliance on the grace of God, is how they have seen transformation and fruit.

What if you are in a community that feels stuck? Learning about change can produce both excitement and frustration. How many leaders long and strive for change in the community under their charge but feel over time that there is so much inertia and hesitancy to change that the community just may never budge? If this is you, you might need to invite God to transform your frustration into godly discontent.

Many pastors and team leaders we've met with over the years have been intimately familiar with the concept of inertia. Inertia, in scientific terms, is the tendency for an object at rest to stay at rest. In spiritual terms it means that we as individuals can get stuck in our lives and in our faith—where there is no growth over time. We get used to the status quo and grow mightily resistant to change.

Not only does this happen with individual Christians, but it also happens to communities of Christians.

Whole communities can grow quite resistant to change. Spiritual inertia settles in, a holy huddle takes over, and the idea of getting such a stuck community unstuck can seem nearly impossible. As spiritual inertia relates to witness, it is not uncommon for a Christian community to get so comfortable that years go by without any real witness happening at all. This is, from a kingdom perspective, a dangerous and sad place to be in. It is reminiscent of the image Jesus painted of the fruitless fig tree in Luke 13. Jesus is responding to people who are spiritually content with themselves and looking down their noses at others. To help them see that they have a drastic need to repent and change, Jesus tells the parable of the fruitless fig tree:

> A man had a fig tree planted in his vineyard; and he came looking for fruit on it and found none. So he said to the gardener, "See here! For three years I have come looking for fruit on this fig tree, and still I find none. Cut it down! Why should it be wasting the soil?" He replied, "Sir, let it alone for one more year, until I dig around it and put manure on it. If it bears fruit next year, well and good; but if not, you can cut it down." (Luke 13:6-9 NRSV)

Ultimately this is a parable about spiritual change within people who need to repent. It is about both God's righteous judgment (the owner is right to judge the tree and remove it from his vineyard) and Jesus' relentless pursuit of those who need to repent (it is beautiful that the gardener holds out hope for the tree and is willing to work on it). While we do not think that Jesus' parable is about leading community-wide change, we do find this image to be striking, memorable, and helpful for those seeking to lead a change process.

Later we will focus more on the roles of the owner and the gardener in the parable, but here we'd like to just pause and consider the dilemma of the fruitless tree. It is, in a sense, a perfect image of a Christian community that is not bearing witness to the gospel and is stuck in that place. Jesus calls his people to be his witnesses, to share the gospel with others, but sometimes that doesn't happen. In that sense leaders of stuck communities are right to feel frustrated. There is not fruit on a tree that was planted specifically to bear fruit. The dilemma of the fruitless tree is a true dilemma that needs to be addressed.

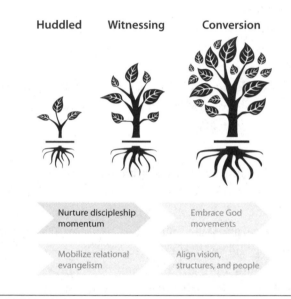

Figure 4.1. Discipleship momentum

This is why we have remained quite attentive to the communities we visit that do experience change. What happened to help a previously stuck community get unstuck? What do the communities who are growing in their witness have in common? In our travels we have heard from others again and again that stuck communities really can get unstuck, that huddled communities really can break the huddle and get involved in witness. It might be surprising in a book about witness, but the best thing we have found to break the huddle is a commitment to practical discipleship. In communities that have broken the huddle there is a discipleship momentum that has been nurtured, in many cases through a commitment to a simple discipleship cycle. There is a way to help a community handle God's Word that predictably results in movement and change within the community. That's what this chapter is all about.

THE DISCIPLESHIP CYCLE

With a name like *the discipleship cycle* you may be tempted to think we're talking about some clever new leadership trick. The truth is, we're talking about something very old and simple: Jesus' plan to transform and move his followers through his words. On many occasions Jesus' words had no effect on his hearers. Just consider how often the Pharisees listened to Jesus teach, and yet they were not moved. The gospels reveal that it is not enough to hear Jesus' words. Jesus explained this phenomenon in detail in the parable of the sower (which perhaps could more aptly be named the parable of the soils).

This parable (found in Matthew 13, Mark 4 and Luke 8) reveals Jesus' clear understanding of how change happens in people. In a sense the parable is shocking: it turns out people are not transformed by what they hear. Growth does not come from studying the Bible alone. According to Jesus, growth occurs as we *respond to* his word. The seed (his words) will fall onto many different types of people—but only those who receive his word and do something with it are the good soil that is changed for the long run.

The parable itself is very simple and well known to most of us, but it's likely that when he first taught it most of the crowd probably wondered why a carpenter was telling them about how to farm. Most of the crowd walks away after this word (seed) from Jesus. They do nothing with it. But a few, his disciples, are confused. Perhaps intrigued. Their response is to wrestle with it and take it to Jesus so that he can explain it. Jesus doesn't sigh at their lack of understanding; rather he celebrates what they've done with his word (wrestling with it). He goes on to explain the entire parable (the seeds are his words, the soils are different ways people respond to his words). The disciples have, in essence, lived out the parable— they took in the word and responded to it, wrestled with it. Jesus actually calls their active response that day the "secret of the kingdom of heaven."

In this parable Jesus gives us insight into how change is possible in us and through us as his disciples: we hear his words, we respond to those words, and we debrief the words/response with others. This communal, responsive handling of God's words is what makes us "good soil" that is transformed because of those words—producing crops. Jesus continually taught his disciples and called them to action. He continually debriefed with them both the words themselves (Jesus often had to help his disciples think about his parables) and their risks of faith in response to his words (Jesus often debriefed their amazing and frustrating mission experiences). And he did all this (the teaching, the call to respond, and the debrief) with them *in community*. It's really very simple. And quite profound. The process of hearing and responding to God's words in community is what makes Christians (and whole Christian communities) grow and move and change. This is precisely what happened at UCSD and can be pictured with a simple hear–respond–debrief image.

This representation of the basic discipleship cycle arose from a community learning process that was actually somewhat reminiscent of the team learning that gave birth to the five thresholds back in the 1990s. A group of InterVarsity staff studied how different leaders developed their teams, and they saw this simple, common pattern. Each person used different language to describe what they did, but the process was very similar. We tested out what we were seeing in different contexts. Was it three steps, four steps, two steps? Thus the discipleship cycle emerged, and we love how God has been using it in our lives and in our communities.[1] Consider the three basic parts of the cycle, shown in figure 4.2.

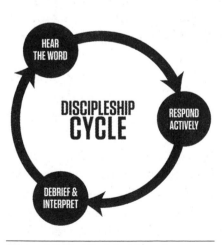

Figure 4.2. The discipleship cycle

Hear the Word. Every sermon or Bible study or time of quiet Bible reading is an adventure. Every time we study the Scripture is an opportunity to be transformed. The discipleship cycle upends our stagnant, safe Christianity. We can hear the Word of God in many ways:

- sermon
- Bible study
- inductive study
- personal devotional
- prayer
- worship
- testimony

Respond. There are many ways to respond to Jesus and the Scriptures. Just as we see in the gospels, people respond to Jesus in a wide variety of contexts and applications. We might cook a meal for someone to show them God's love, we might invite someone to repent of sin in their personal life, we might invite others to speak into our lives about an important decision we need to make. We can respond to the Word in many ways.

- serve
- risk
- pray
- reconcile
- cross cultures
- tell our story
- give
- repent
- take a leadership role
- share the gospel

- speak the truth in love to someone
- forgive
- ask questions
- ask for help

Debrief. Why is it important to debrief what we've heard and what we've done? Consider the disciples and the Parable of the Sower again: the disciples' eyes are opened as they debrief Jesus' teaching with him. It is significant that Jesus didn't say that *hearing his words* was the secret of the kingdom, but he sees the disciples' questions to him *about his words* in response as being the secret of the kingdom.

Debriefing is a communal activity. It is a practical step of humility to admit that we do not yet really understand what God just did or what God is trying to get through our thick skulls and hard hearts. Debriefing creates the space for a deeper layer of understanding and growth. And community is the place where this happens, whether we're debriefing with a small group, a spouse, a friend, or a group of strangers we circle up with after a worship service.

A debrief can help us exercise wisdom about what we are hearing in the Scripture. This can help us avoid misreading or misapplying what we've read. All three of us have embarrassing personal stories of times we genuinely attempted to apply what we had read in Scripture but did so without wisdom or discernment. Debriefing with others can help us avoid such situations. If you read the Word and respond but do not debrief, it can lead to activism and impulse, not transformation. It is a life of busyness with good things but an inability to understand what the goal of the activity is about. For some, debriefing may feel like you are slowing down. It is indeed a slowing down to pause and learn. In the business world there is the phrase "go slow to go fast." This is what we believe happens in a good debrief. Slow down to reflect and glean the learning. In doing so, growth, change, and integration of the learning into your daily life actually happens more quickly.

Good debriefs access our minds, hearts, and actions. Part of debriefing is gaining deeper understanding about God, evangelism, our mission as witnesses, and ourselves. Capturing these lessons is part of how we mature in our faith. Another part of debriefing is understanding what God might be doing in us. How has the Scripture and our response reoriented our hearts toward something new?

The last part of debriefing can affect the actions we take next. Based on what happened in me, in our community, or with my non-Christian friend, what is the next conversation, invitation, or step God might be inviting me to take for the sake of what *he* is doing? As a group of people take seriously the discipleship cycle and respond in faith to the nonbelievers God has placed in their lives, there is individual transformation for the believer and the community as a whole. The believer begins to recognize what God is doing in him, and the community begins to recognize God's corporate work. (See appendix D, "Leading Better Debriefs.")

We can debrief in many ways:

- pray
- ponder
- reflect
- journal
- sit down and have coffee together
- pause in the middle of worship
- send a text to a friend
- celebrate
- expect to be changed by God
- seek an interpretation
- tell a story
- ask questions

We have seen this pattern help communities move from huddled to witnessing. There is something transformational about hearing the Word in community, choosing to do something as an individual or a group in response, and then coming back together to debrief and gain more understanding about God and his words, more understanding about ourselves, and more understanding about the community. This is even more true when the response to the Word is engaging nonbelievers on their spiritual journey. We have found that hear–respond–debrief is a helpful pattern for discipleship.

In fact, wherever we've seen real community-wide change, when we stop to scratch beneath the surface and find out what makes that community tick, we find the same thing: a community that is wrestling with God's Word together, responding to his Word together, and honestly talking with each other about the hearing and responding that they've done.

Although we have shared the cycle in the order hear–respond–debrief, you can begin anywhere in the pattern. Sometimes the pattern starts during the response or debrief. This was true for Susan, who went on a service project hosted by the college she attended, which involved putting a roof on a school. While serving with her friends who did not share her faith, she realized that they were not as far from God as she once thought. As she was reflecting on this, it occurred to her that their hearts were in the right place—committed to the poor, to seeking justice, to loving and serving a broken world. This led her to invite them to study Scripture with her because she wanted them to know that those desires came from God and that Jesus wanted those same things too. In this case the order was respond–debrief–hear.

For me (Val), the cycle often starts with a debrief. God uses my times of reflection on what I am feeling, thinking, and experiencing. Sometimes God uses these moments of debrief to prompt me to some sort of response: to call or visit or bring a meal to someone, which leads me to pray and offer a word of hope from Scripture. Sometimes these moments of debriefing bring me to Scripture and prayer as I sense God inviting me to find my story in his story, and that leads me to respond in faith. Debrief–respond–hear. It doesn't matter the order, but we have found that it is most helpful to complete all three steps in the cycle.

In addition to the general way of seeing the world and responding to God's Word in our lives, this becomes the very way of moving communities outward. This simple discipleship cycle is what makes a community movable, pliable, and open to change. (Nothing else seems to get whole communities moving in this way: not an evangelistic program, not hiring an evangelist, not laying on a guilt trip.) This isn't just what made movement possible in the UCSD fellowship, but it is how communities are intended to be changed by Jesus and his Word. Consider what our friend Geoff experienced.

GEOFF AND THE PUTTING-IT-INTO-ACTION GROUP

Geoff has always loved applying Scripture. He himself was transformed not just by hearing the Word but by doing something with what he heard. When Geoff became a small group leader, people liked his approach to studying the Scripture together, but the application tended toward privatized and individualistic baby steps. Like Ryan, Geoff had his own season of godly discontent. Couldn't the Bible be more impactful on people's lives?

When Geoff first started working with a group of freshmen at Boston College, the community was a wonderful huddle. They loved God and each other well. The vision that Geoff used to rally the huddle around was "let's become fringe centric." To him this meant that he wanted visitors to walk into the community and feel like they belonged. Geoff saw the faith of the huddle and saw how serious they were about studying Scripture. They seemed captivated by Scripture and applying it in very practical ways, so Geoff invited them to form a new kind of small group, a "putting-it-into-action" group. He told them, "For the next few months, let's get together weekly to discuss fairly straightforward passages from the four Gospels and then brainstorm specific action steps that we will actually commit to doing. The following week each of us will share what we tried, what happened, and what we saw God do."

This probably sounds simple, but in practice it is very different from just studying the Bible in order to be edified or inspired. Often application can be vague at the end of a small group or sermon. Not for Geoff and this putting-it-into-action group. They never left off with, "Go and do something if you feel like God is putting it on your heart." Instead it was clear: "Let's decide what we want to do." They left very clear about what they were committing to do in the coming week.

The first couple responses to the Word were low-risk, like doing something in secret in response to Matthew 6 (do not let the left hand know what the right hand is doing), or taking a friend out for coffee or a meal and asking about their faith background and what it means to them today. Later the challenges were more risky, like sharing your story about why you believe with a friend or inviting your friend to a community gathering. The group was amazed by what they saw happening in each other and what was happening with each other's friends. Students like Rachel, Chris, and Eric talked about what God was doing in them through these challenges, how they felt like they were growing in their faith.

Most of the challenges (see appendix E for practical challenges from the putting-it-into-action group) had something to do with people, which began to shape how the community talked about their friends, most of whom were not following Jesus. Everyone in the study began to look at their friends differently, yearning for them to experience the kind of love they had. This putting-it-into-action group helped all of them become witnesses. They took risks to serve others not just by acts of service but with their words. They learned to share their own stories of faith. They asked their friends questions about their spiritual backgrounds so that they could understand where they were coming from. Matt and Sarah helped their friends learn about Jesus by leading Bible studies from the gospels. They didn't have the language at the time, but they were meandering through the five thresholds with people, and God was working in both subtle and obvious ways.

After this crash course on applying Scripture, they were different. They didn't want to go back to just reading the Bible but not doing it. The members were so affected by the Bible that they spontaneously started Bible studies with their other friends—an even larger thing was happening in the community. The whole community talked about what was happening in this one pocket of the community and became curious about these challenges. A huddled community was becoming a witnessing community because of God working through their discipleship cycle.

NURTURING DISCIPLESHIP MOMENTUM

What it looks like to implement a basic discipleship cycle depends quite a bit on context. We've seen discipleship cycles implemented using small groups, sermons, classes, and mentoring relationships.

Small groups. In the work we've done on college campuses with student groups (where small groups are the strongest delivery method for Scripture), a small group–based approach has worked quite effectively. In a small group you have a community that regularly reads and studies Scripture—that's the *hearing* part. It is noteworthy that these are not groups that read books (like the one you are holding) but who read the Bible. Hearing God's Word is the key here.

And anytime you equip small group leaders to purposefully integrate some sort of application to the Scripture—that's the *responding* part. These can be individual applications or a group application. The important point is that responding to God's Word (not just reading and enjoying it) is assumed.

Finally, small group leaders can be trained to always circle back (perhaps at the beginning of the next study) to debrief what has been heard and done in response. This final step is absolutely key and often forgotten because the leader is so eager to move on to the next passage to be studied. Debriefing is important on one level because it shows everyone that the responding really is important. (We always *inspect* what we *expect*—if you never talk about your responses, the subtle message is that responding to Scripture isn't as important as hearing it and studying it.) In addition, debriefing the Word has a way of massaging it deeper into our hearts and lives.

Sermons. We are huge fans of sermons. The three of us are all preachers and believe in the public heralding of God's Word. But we also recognize that it is tempting in some contexts for Christians to sit passively and listen to a sermon and then head out to get lunch and tackle the new week before them—without a single look back at the Word they heard preached. If you wonder if this is the temptation in your community, just ask a number of people midweek what last Sunday's sermon was about. (For those of us who spend so much time carefully writing, crafting, and delivering these sermons, it can be humbling to hear how quickly the Word preached can fade.)

So how can we fight against the sermon fade? How do we encourage people to not just *hear* the Word during a sermon but then take the next step to *respond* to that Word and *debrief* it with others? We have seen this successfully accomplished in a number of ways:

- worship bulletins with ample space for taking notes (at Don's church they put three sections for taking notes: Hear—what stood out in the text from today; Respond—what are you going to do this week because of what you heard?; and Debrief—who are you going to debrief with this week?)

- application questions printed in the bulletin or available online based on the sermon just preached

- in-worship opportunities to process and debrief with others (like taking three minutes to turn and answer a specific question with a few people around you)

- sermon-based small groups or classes that spend more time on the week's text

- CDs or online versions of sermons made available after a retreat or worship service for people to listen again to the message or share it with others

- testimonies shared with the whole group from people who have applied and debriefed the Word with others—as a way of celebrating and illustrating the discipleship cycle

Creating space for community-wide active responses sometimes means we reverse the order in how we plan our events. Consider our friend Steven. Steven spoke at Northern Arizona University about how to tell your faith story in a way that is winsome, intelligible, and brief. But he did not just want to inspire and have it go nowhere. How can we create an opportunity to equip these folks on the spot if they want to live into this teaching? At the end of the talk, Steven gave this invitation:

> Let's have a moment to check in with God. If you feel like God is *stirring* you to make this a priority, we would like to help make that possible. We have prepared a twenty-minute seminar right now for you to get equipped and take a practical step. The seminar is right over there, directly behind this room. In a second, I am going to invite those who want to get out of their seats and get some quick training to head over to that option.

Maybe fifty students did exactly that, even some first-time visitors. As the worship team led those who stayed behind in a final song, the rest were learning practical ways to see their story more clearly and to share it more fruitfully. In fact, Val and Doug had previously helped train other emerging leaders to be the ones to run the seminar. Everyone was trying something new and taking faith risks that evening, even us! (In the past, our training sessions were at least an hour long, usually on the weekend. This old way of approaching training meant only the most committed attended and were helped. By shifting how we think about training, we can offer a condensed version to a greater number of potential witnesses.)

Since many Christian communities already have some weekly sermon built in, it can be a strategic place to make a few small adjustments to begin nurturing discipleship momentum rather than just sermon listening.

Classes and mentoring relationships. Every community is different in how they pursue growth as Christians. Some communities have a real appreciation for classes and deep learning. Other communities highly value mentoring relationships—making sure that everyone in the church is being mentored and is mentoring another in discipleship relationships. No matter what model a church or community has, it can at times be shifted or tweaked to make sure that the whole discipleship cycle is happening. Rather than reinvent the wheel and implement a brand new structure in a church, it is possible to leverage what is already in place to start creating momentum and change through the power of God's Word handled in community.

It is true, also, that some communities can get so stuck that they need more of a shakeup, and implementing a new structure might be necessary. But no matter what strategic and tactical moves a leader makes to help nurture discipleship momentum, it is God's Word that is key. Jesus, who knew his followers better than they knew themselves, was very clear that his words (the seed) can create great change when they are received and responded to.

If a leader wants to see change happen in a specific area (for example, see a community grow specifically in its witness), then clearly Scriptures about God's good news, how he calls his followers to share that news, etc. are apropos texts to feed into a community's discipleship cycles.

REAL CHANGE IS POSSIBLE

We have found the discipleship cycle to be a helpful pattern to help people and communities change. This is especially significant when we consider the kind of community-wide change we are focusing on in *Breaking the Huddle*—change that results in Christians being used by God to introduce their friends to Jesus.

We believe that the transformation that happened for Ryan's community and Geoff's community is possible for every community as we respond to Jesus' Parable of the Sower by receiving and doing something with his Word—and by doing that in community with others (see figure 4.3). This simple discipleship cycle is like a grease that can get stuck communities moving again. The beautiful thing is that change and movement are not precipitated by human effort or dazzling inspirational speeches or jaw-dropping programs—they are fueled by the words of Jesus. This is how Jesus knew his disciples would "produce great crops."

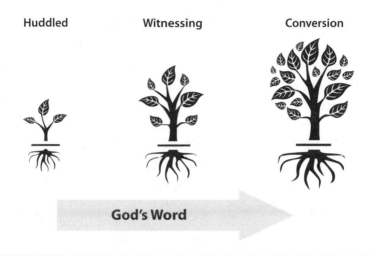

| Huddled | Witnessing | Conversion |

God's Word

Figure 4.3. God's Word transforming communities

This is great news because while it is true that our flesh and the enemy are conspiring to create a sort of evangelism entropy (slowly lowering our communities' witness temperatures over time), it is equally true that to hear the Word of God, respond to it, and debrief it with others creates movement in the opposite direction. It gets a group moving, making it possible for a group's witness temperature to get warmer. Whether your community is huddled and you'd love to see it become witnessing or whether your community is already witnessing but you have a heart to grow red-hot in your witness, you can know that real change is possible where disciples are hearing–responding–debriefing.

Without a basic discipleship cycle, it appears to us that sustained, community-wide transformation is quite unlikely. Certainly we've seen groups that get "fired up" for evangelism after a conference or sermon series or book study and even busy themselves with evangelistic activity. But if hearts have not been truly changed and moved by God's Word, genuine, sustainable witness doesn't tend to happen. Duty and excitement and guilt and groupthink can only take you so far. Real change, as Jesus so beautifully illustrated, happens as we hear–respond–debrief. This is the case no matter what type of community you lead, but this is perhaps especially salient when it comes to leading a huddled community.

The discipleship cycle can help a huddled community move toward becoming a witnessing community because it helps us break out of a static or cerebral version of being a disciple. The cycle gets us out of our pews and into people's lives. It has movement. It helps us expect God to speak today.

This is the first place I (Val) started as I tried to put into practice the lessons I learned from UCSD. In order for any community to change, the people need to hear from God about why this change is needed, and they need to see a picture of what the change could look like. It was tempting to just try to do all the same programs that UCSD was doing or give all the same sermons or plan the same events. But in the end I knew God needed to orchestrate this change, not me. I wanted others to be inspired and curious about what God had in mind for faith communities and to ask him what he had in mind for our community. The discipleship cycle ensured that I was never getting ahead of the group or God in my desire (and my angst) for change. It allowed God's Word to be the hope we clung to the most as we sought to become a witnessing community.

PRAYER

Father, we believe that your Word is vibrant, powerful, and able to bring the dead to life. We believe that your Word deserves our active response. Help me to pay attention to your nudging when I am reading Scripture or listening to a sermon. I long to be a doer of the Word and not merely a hearer. As a community, give us trusting and obedient hearts to respond when you speak. Give us courage to love in risky ways. Help us to learn from our experiences. We want to be a community that looks like and lives like Jesus. Help us not be afraid to get practical in our responses. Amen.

DISCUSSION

1. What do you like about the putting-it-into-action story? What are one or two ideas that you might like to try out in your own small group?

2. Val shared about her feelings of jealousy and skepticism as she learned about other people's witnessing communities. What are some feelings that you are having as you also hear about other people's growing communities?

3. What do you like about the discipleship cycle? Which step of the cycle is your community strongest in? Weakest in? How might you use the discipleship cycle more fruitfully in your community?

5

MOBILIZE RELATIONAL EVANGELISM

Before I ever met Doug or Don, I (Val) belonged to a very huddled community of students. This wasn't just metaphorical but literal—we literally hid out in a very spooky, secluded room. We made jokes about meeting in the early Christian catacombs in the dark basement of the chapel. And the truth is, we really liked being huddled. We liked not being seen. We were both an intimate huddle and a defensive huddle. We were "the few, the proud," and all ten of us were committed to helping each other keep our faith alive. We existed for ourselves.

The decision to leave the chapel and move our meetings to the student center was a huge risk. For as long as this particular community had existed, they had met in the chapel basement. But we made the move to the student center, and we decided to structure the meetings so that there was ample time to get to know people, have fun, and have good conversation. Our group grew a lot that year in size. Many people showed up because they had friends in the group or found our group to be friendly and fun. We became much better at building trust and even cultivating curiosity as a group. But that was about it. One person made a decision to follow

Jesus that year, but we didn't even know it until the end of the year when she said, "I think I became a Christian this year." I was thrilled she had made this kind of commitment, but it seemed wrong that this miracle would happen without anyone even knowing. God had moved powerfully among us, and we didn't even notice. That was a turning point in my life.

As I shared in the first chapter, witness used to be a concept for me, not a lifestyle. Good evangelism was elusive and confusing for me. But around this time I came across an article that Doug had written about the five thresholds—the very article that would later be the impetus for the book *I Once Was Lost.* That article became my new best friend. I read and reread that article. In fact, I picked up the phone and called Doug, and that was the first time we ever talked. I was ready to learn. (Ironically, Doug doesn't even remember me calling him.) On that call I asked him for more specifics about what exactly you ask a curious person whom you are trying to help become open to change. I asked Doug and other people who had evangelism gifts for these kinds of nitty-gritty specifics. The framework of the five thresholds was interesting to me, but it was utterly useless if I didn't know how to use it well with my community. (That's why when *I Once Was Lost* was published I read it three times and then bought a case of the books to give out to three different leadership teams so we could discuss it!)

In the beginning I just mimicked what others told me. And lo and behold, I started to have good conversations with non-Christians. I trained others in exactly the way I was mimicking the "experts." The feedback was that as we all took baby steps, we were getting better at having conversations about faith. Eventually the thresholds got inside my head, they became more intuitive for me, and I developed my own style. I discovered Val-flavored questions that I would use to instigate meaningful conversations. It would be fair to say that over time the thresholds have shaped my worldview. Other people I have trained would say the same happened for them.

But in the beginning, we were all mimicking other people and praying like crazy that somehow God would use these borrowed words to help move people toward Jesus. Though we didn't have the language for it at the time, I realize now that our move from huddled to witnessing was strengthened as we took steps in what I would come to know as *relational evangelism*. It turns out that is a key component of moving from huddled to witnessing.

The move from huddled to witnessing is the natural, embedded nature of the kingdom of God. In God's kingdom his right hand is moving, drawing people to him, so of course his people are getting caught up in that great work of homecoming. God moments have a way of leading to other God moments.

Consider what naturally happens (without any explicit leadership from God's people) with the woman at the well. She has a life-altering God moment when Jesus engages her in conversation. Then, without any prompting from Jesus or the disciples, she drops her bucket, runs back into her village, and starts telling other people what has happened to her. Then (while the disciples are still stuck on their own small agendas, as we've seen) the spark of her God moment begins to spread into a wildfire of curiosity, and the whole town draws near to Jesus. All this without any disciple-led strategies or programs or exertion of leadership. If you are in a huddled community and are hoping for change, the good news is that God is the one who moves, and when he does, things can take off!

Of course, we cannot summon God moments like you summon a butler or a waiter at a restaurant. But we do know that God is seeking to save the lost (see Luke 19:10). And when his right hand moves, that starts a beautiful kind of momentum all on its own. We have seen one person in a community be transformed by a God moment, followed by a godly jealousy infecting the others in the group. They want what God just gave their friend. They wonder what God might do in their own lives. These God moments begin to shape the expectations and culture of the community. People begin to turn their eyes outward to see more of what God is doing outside their community and to discern how their community might intentionally seek to serve. We have seen one incredible God moment really spark and change an entire community.

The good news is that God is still on the move. And God moments are infectious. There is a beautiful momentum that is native to the kingdom of God. So if it is all about God, what role do we play?

LEADERSHIP AND WITNESS

Was Jesus satisfied with having a God moment with the woman at the well and then sitting back to see what would happen? No. Jesus began immediately to invite his disciples into this God moment with him. Were they willing colaborers with him? Not on this day. But that did not stop Jesus; he worked with the disciples to help them see their own role in this great kingdom work and to inspire them to live into their roles. Given how remarkable the story of the woman and her village is, it is meaningful how much of John's narrative focuses on Jesus and his work with the reticent disciples.

The reality is that leadership matters. And this is especially true when it comes to pursuing community-wide change in a group. Just as Jesus invited his disciples to enter into this kingdom expansion work, he invites leaders of every age to labor in God's great work with him—to call the Christians in our age and in our communities to be about the work of witness. We are called to lead in such a way that the communities we lead are growing in witness over time.

But how do you do that? Specifically, how do you help a community that doesn't have a lot of experience with witness start to get involved with sharing the good news? How do you help the huddled communities we looked at in chapter one become more like the witnessing communities we looked at in chapter two?

Undoubtedly you have thought of a variety of microstrategies and ideas as you have read through the three stages of witnessing communities:

- Huddled communities have the habit of avoiding deep relationships with "outsiders." How can I encourage and nurture and celebrate these kinds of relationships?

- Witnessing communities expect God moments. What are ways we can stoke that kind of expectancy?

- Huddled communities typically focus on their internal needs. How can I help turn the eyes of our folks towards others' needs?

- Witnessing communities tend to "sing glad songs of salvation." Where can we fit stories of change into our worship services?

We think that an honest conversation exploring these questions should help your community make progress from huddled to witnessing.

Also, the discipleship cycle is a true macrostrategy that really can be purposefully implemented and really does create momentum in any community.

But in addition to all that, there is another macrostrategy that we have seen church after church successfully pursue to help their whole community move from huddled to willing: mobilizing relational evangelism (see figure 5.1). That's what this chapter will explore.

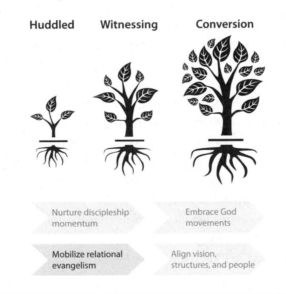

| Huddled | Witnessing | Conversion |

Nurture discipleship momentum

Embrace God movements

Mobilize relational evangelism

Align vision, structures, and people

Figure 5.1. Mobilizing relational evangelism

MOBILIZING RELATIONAL EVANGELISM

Is relational evangelism the only way to share the gospel? Absolutely not. Is relational evangelism a biblical approach to sharing the good news that happens to be perfectly fitted for the age we live in? Absolutely. And it is a quite fruitful approach as well.

In *I Once Was Lost* we explored the various ways that distrust of Christians marks the age we live in. This high degree of distrust helps explain why so many non-Christians' paths to Jesus begin in earnest when they start to trust one Christian. The gospel wants to be shared within the light and warmth of friendship. Research also indicates that those who come to faith in the context of a friendship are much more likely to persevere and grow in the faith than those who come to faith through a program or event alone. This isn't to say that real evangelism never takes place outside the context of real relationships, but there is something wise and strategic about mobilizing relational evangelism in a church community. We may pine for a former age when trust was high and biblical sermons and speeches alone were enough to help people come to Jesus, but that simply is not the age we live in.

Although the article on the five thresholds was first written nearly twenty years ago, this relational approach has not faded out like most of the other fads we tried in the 1990s. In fact, the concept of the thresholds is bearing fruit in unexpected places and in mysterious ways as people are encouraged to build trust and honor the process non-Christians are in. Mobilizing relational evangelism really works!

For example, the thresholds are bearing fruit among graduate students and faculty in secular colleges and universities. Grad students have identified with the journey and the language. In the past, the stereotype of Christian grad students and faculty who study and work in secular universities was that they had to keep their faith to themselves or else lose their jobs. But today, by God's grace, God is using the five thresholds to empower them to talk more freely about God's work in their lives. We are seeing profound transformation and conversions across the country, as huddled communities in departments become witnessing communities.

Our friend Melodie is a regional director for graduate student and faculty ministry with InterVarsity Christian Fellowship. She is a big fan of the thresholds. Here is her take:

A huge part of what makes the thresholds so significant in our GFM [Graduate and Faculty Ministries] context is the fact that they are relationally based. Starting with trust, then cultivating curiosity, etc. Many grad students and faculty are terrified (I don't think that's too strong of a word!) that they might be asked a question that they cannot answer, so they avoid bringing up faith related topics. The beauty of the thresholds (once the penny drops for people) is that they don't have to "know the right answer" for every question—but can actually build trust through the simple act of exploring answers together![1]

Beth Ann is a PhD student in history at a secular university. She recently went through training on the five thresholds. What was her reaction? The very first thing she wanted to do afterwards was to share the thresholds with others. God was using it to set something free inside of her.

The five thresholds are also finding traction internationally. We have heard back repeatedly, "This is not just for the United States. The thresholds are very transferable and universal." The thresholds are bearing fruit in the former Soviet Union, the Middle East, and even in a few corners of Europe and Asia. Relational evangelism works in multiple cultural contexts.

Maybe most surprising and delightful has been to hear how non-Christians themselves like the five thresholds. As we have used the threshold tools among communities of curious people, they find our terms aspirational and safe. They want to trust. They want to be curious. Being open is a winsome concept. Becoming a seeker is how they want to see themselves. They self-select, and the five categories help them grow. Non-Christians do not know how to journey toward Jesus, and for many this basic outline has not only resonated in an aspirational way, but it has also given non-Christians a basic contour for exploring the faith.

Take our friends Jamie and Angela, for example. They live in Kansas and had done an amazing job of building trust and stoking curiosity among a group of non-Christian international students. So Angela invited them to form a small group with her to explore Jesus. The group engaged well with the passages about Jesus. But Angela's suggestions for active response and applying the Word just weren't resonating with these international students. So Angela asked Jamie for help. She felt stuck and discontent. Jamie and Angela decided to hang out with the international students outside of the small group time. They saw that the group collaborated well together when it came to other settings. So Angela and Jamie wondered, *Why is this not happening in the small group?* The small group time felt like a group of individuals suffering alone through this mystery of finding faith.

So what did they do? Jamie suggested to Angela that they use the last six weeks of school to do video training on the five thresholds with the international students. Angela was understandably hesitant. *Why would you train non-Christians in the five thresholds? You can't train non-Christians in evangelism!* But they did show the videos and, by God's grace, the international students had big light bulb moments during both the *curiosity* and the *openness* sessions. They all self-identified in one of these two thresholds. So Angela asked them, "What would it take for you to move on to the next threshold?" They began to offer each other suggestions for how they might become more open or even become seekers. This group of people who were individuals thinking about faith had morphed into a team, a community of friends helping each other take practical steps through the thresholds. This amazing process was relational at its core.

Later, Angela invited one of these students, Raman, to the Urbana missions conference as an opportunity for him to spend a week seeking Jesus directly. She focused his quest, asking him to name his most pressing question. He replied, "Can I meet God?" What an outstanding question! In the prayer room at Urbana, Raman did meet God; he was healed physically, emotionally, and spiritually, and he crossed over the fifth threshold—he became a follower! At the time of this book publishing, Raman has returned to his small group and is passionately helping the others become seekers as well. This is evangelism that is relational.

Our research in *I Once Was Lost* and our time working with leaders and evangelists and a variety of Christian communities have all underscored just how powerful and beautiful and effective it is to mobilize relational evangelism.

TRUST   CURIOSITY   CHANGE   SEEKING   FOLLOWER

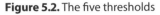

Figure 5.2. The five thresholds

There are downsides to this macrostrategy, of course. It is much easier and more efficient to just plan an evangelistic event, for example, than it is to inspire, equip, and mobilize Christians to be engaged in relational evangelism right where they live and work and play. The former just requires some money and some decent organizers. The latter requires heart change, modeling, risk-taking, and confrontation with our own flesh and its apathies and fears. Relational evangelism is messy and hard.

But the upsides are unbelievable. The more witnessing communities we hang out in, the more we see how perfectly fitted this strategy is not only for the age we live in but also for the task of helping a community move from huddled to witnessing. This is true, in part, because relational evangelism confronts all three huddled habits. As you'll recall, huddled communities focus on their own needs, have limited energy for deep relationships with outsiders, and view witness as special. Pursuing relational evangelism directly counteracts each of these habits: it forces a community to think about the needs of real people who really don't know Jesus, it calls Christians to actively pursue building and nurturing relationships explicitly with outsiders, and it shatters the myth that evangelism is something for the special elite forces to do. It provides a vision and path of witness that is possible for everyone.

Not only does relational evangelism confront all three huddled habits, it also helps cultivate all three witnessing habits: expecting God moments, recognizing God moments, and responding to God moments. Relational evangelism as a strategy forces Christians to consider their friendships, workplaces, walks through the neighborhood, time in line at a store, study groups, etc. as places where God might be at work. This cultivates a palpable sense of expectation: God moments could happen anywhere—not just at church or at a huge evangelistic event.

Equipping people for relational evangelism necessarily involves training people to understand how God meets people and begins to draw them into his kingdom. This heightened, more nuanced understanding about how people journey toward Jesus naturally causes believers to become more attentive to the different parts of their friends' journeys—they become more able and willing to recognize God moments when they happen. And a community that is trained and equipped specifically for relational evangelism will understand how to respond *not perfectly* but *in the moment* to potential God moments.

While there are a variety of effective tactics that can be used to mobilize relational evangelism, the five thresholds are a useful tool. Certainly this is not the only way to inspire and equip a church for relational evangelism, but we do know that it is an effective and fruitful one. It involves three different steps.

STEP 1: INTRODUCE A COMMUNITY TO THE FIVE THRESHOLDS

Writing *I Once Was Lost* was our way of offering more widely this wisdom tool derived from the testimonies of brand-new Christians, but more of our time in recent years has been spent introducing the five thresholds to churches, student fellowships, mission agencies, and denominations one at a time. The consistent feedback we get is that this tool

- helps people understand their non-Christian friends better, replacing frustration and confusion with empathy;

- is freeing and motivating, relieving much of the stress people have felt about being a witness;

- makes people feel empowered and equipped, rather than inadequate; and

- gives their whole community a common language and strategy for pursuing evangelism.

It has been a joy to watch various communities move from huddled to witnessing by introducing the five thresholds. But it needs to be acknowledged that this isn't without pain. Huddled communities have some natural objections and hesitancies when it comes to relational evangelism. The good news is, we've seen how introducing the five thresholds helps overcome those initial reactions.

Because huddled communities are focused on their own needs, a call to relational evangelism usually is perceived as a threat. It's a threat to time, to resources, and to existing programs. Internal needs can make people tightfisted when it comes to a call to focus on the needs of the lost who aren't even in the church.

But one of the great features of the five thresholds is how it helps us understand non-Christians more clearly. Rather than a purely conceptual or theological call to evangelism (which can be fairly easy to dodge), the five thresholds puts flesh on the journeys of the real people around us. Empathy is built. And empathy stokes our love and concern. Helping a congregation stop to actually think in detail about non-Christians has a way of fanning into flame a genuine concern and love for them. Suddenly your own internal concerns aren't the only concerns on your landscape anymore. This genuine, personal love and interest in non-Christians is often more motivating than the most powerful of sermons.

But huddled communities aren't just preoccupied with internal concerns; they also tend to avoid relationships with outsiders. There are various reasons why this is the case, but it does lead to a genuine allergy to any call to relational evangelism. While doing training on the five thresholds in churches, we have seen individuals really push back against the idea of relational evangelism in a Q&A time (for a variety of thoughtful, high-minded reasons) only to find out later in personal conversation that their real hesitancy comes from their embarrassment that they aren't friends with any non-Christians. To someone without a genuine, trusting relationship with a non-Christian, relational evangelism can feel impossible.

But here's the thing about the five thresholds: they reveal a natural path that always begins with trust building. We've seen people who were stressed (because they initially assumed we were inviting them to force awkwardly religious and random conversations on their friends) become relaxed and freed when they realize that what's most helpful to non-Christians, is actually quite doable. And even folks with no real relationships with non-Christians realize that they are in the game too. To begin to build a genuine relationship with someone is relational evangelism. There's something very freeing about this realization. Relational evangelism is a game anyone can play.

Of course that idea is new to many people. Often in huddled churches evangelism is seen as a special, tricky task reserved for the few, the proud, the professional evangelists and pastors. And if the only way to be a witness were to give a persuasive evangelistic talk, then there would be some real weight to this belief. But the five thresholds disabuse us of that notion. Knowing the basic contours of the path people tend to walk toward Jesus is quite empowering. It helps us have a basic sense of how to be helpful to our friends. If they're at threshold #1, we endeavor to slowly build trust. If they are at threshold #2, we look for ways to pique their curiosity about Jesus. (Forcing random religious conversations upon people rarely piques their interest in Jesus.) This wisdom tool helps people realize and experience how accessible this really is for everyone. It's one thing to hear Jesus invite us to be salt and light. It's another thing to feel equipped to actually do it.

There are practical ways to introduce a community to the five thresholds. We've been contacted by churches and fellowships around the country and around the world who've tried these methods:

- used *I Once Was Lost* in all their small groups
- offered training on the five thresholds for their leadership retreat
- developed a sermon series with the five thresholds embedded
- held an all-church weekend conference to do the training
- used video and media resources to train their evangelism leaders
- created visuals, models, and tools (based on the five thresholds) for their staff training geared specifically for their own mission agency
- created testimonial videos for each of the five thresholds and used them in worship

We have been unapologetic and free in helping others learn about this wisdom tool because we sincerely believe we have been handed something solid and true and genuinely helpful by those thousands of new believers who shared their stories with us. We have seen again and again how introducing the five thresholds helps mobilize a community for relational evangelism. But introducing the tool isn't enough. You then need to apply it in personal relationships.

STEP 2: APPLY THE FIVE THRESHOLDS IN PERSONAL RELATIONSHIPS

When we introduce the five thresholds to a new community we are very careful to turn the conversation from conceptual to practical as soon as we can. Don does an exercise with churches called "Me and My Two Friends" where he asks everyone to think of the two non-Christians they are closest to and try to discern where they are on their journey. As awkward as it can feel at first to place a friend somewhere from one to five, there is a moment in this exercise where people move from engaging a concept to prayerfully considering a friend. And prayerfully considering a friend may sound simple, but it is the cornerstone of mobilizing people for relational evangelism.

The beauty about what our friends have taught us is that it recognizes the whole process. Learning an apologetic answer to a tricky question (for example, Why does God allow evil to exist?) is a great thing to learn—but can only be applied if you have a friend asking that question. Learning how to winsomely explain who Jesus is and what he did on the cross is a fabulous tool to add to your tool bag—but you can't necessarily act on it unless you have a trusting friend who is curious about Jesus or your faith.

But the five thresholds model is immediately usable. Even if you aren't in a trusting relationship with a single non-Christian, you can begin to apply what you've learned. You can take actual steps in being a relational witness—even if that means just taking steps in slowly building trust with people. This is a tool that helps us discern where our friends are and how we can come alongside them there. This means we can all start moving, all start engaging in the profound kingdom work of helping people come home to Jesus. And that is the definition of mobilizing people.

I (Don) have had the privilege of not only helping lead Alpha courses at Bonhomme, but also training churches who are implementing Alpha for the first time or have been running courses for a long time but are struggling to get new folks to attend. This has been a fascinating laboratory for seeing how churches engage in relational evangelism. Alpha is a practical introduction to Christianity that involves dinner, a talk about Jesus, and a discussion over dessert with your table mates. Alpha is all about the questions people bring with them—it is an open environment where people can be wherever they are. Because relationships and process are so central to Alpha, it is proving enormously successful in helping churches move from huddled to witnessing.

Based on the stories various Alpha leaders have told me, it appears that many churches that start an Alpha course have great success for three to five years, but then attendance tends to drop off. Non-Christians stop coming. Why is this? It seems that since Alpha is a great place to bring a friend who is curious about the faith or asking questions, when a church starts offering the course there is a wonderful initial harvest of non-Christians coming. After that initial run, folks in the church are still eager for their friends to come, but fewer of those friends actually do.

This is why Alpha initially contacted me to ask about the potential application of the five thresholds among churches. And members of churches are realizing that it actually takes a bit of journeying (say, thresholds one and two) before someone is ready for an Alpha course. They've been actively inviting but haven't known exactly how to journey with a friend pre-Alpha. The fruit these churches have seen in applying the five thresholds to their relationships has been encouraging, and this is a key part in mobilizing any church for relational evangelism. But there's another step that can be taken to fully mobilize, inspire, and equip a congregation for relational evangelism: applying the five thresholds to programs and events.

STEP 3: APPLY THE FIVE THRESHOLDS TO PROGRAMS AND EVENTS

The Alpha course is a good example of how relational evangelism can at times involve programs and events. As you journey with a friend, there are times when the right event or the right program to attend with them is actually really helpful. This is an example of how leaders can develop programs that help people do relational evangelism rather than develop programs that are seen as the evangelism answer. The difference may sound subtle, but it is essential to grasp.

Things get problematic when we see an event as our macrostrategy for witness. How many of us have gone down that path (with eager volunteers, sacrificial hours of labor, great advertising) only to realize when few people show up that it's a rare non-Christian who will come to an event because of a sign. Most non-Christians come to evangelistic events on the arms of a friend. The right event or program can actually help someone journey with a friend, giving them a tangible step to invite their friend to and providing grist for conversation afterwards.

This is why it is essential that we leaders carefully craft these programs and events with non-Christians in mind. This is where applying the insights of the five thresholds to our programs and events becomes so helpful. And exciting!

APPLYING THE FIVE THRESHOLDS TO A RETREAT

Eighteen years ago I (Doug) experienced how helpful this could be when my good friend John Teter and I decided to create a retreat using the insights we had gained from the five thresholds. (The year before we had led a relatively fruitless retreat for seekers, where it seemed the conversations were meandering all over the place.) This is the same retreat where Eddie and Oscar decided to follow Jesus, the story we told you in chapter three. Eddie and Oscar were some of the fruit of the changes we made.

John and I created a separate track for a student retreat for people who were either curious or seekers. Our community had already morphed from witnessing to conversion. We had started to see the number of people who were making decisions to follow Jesus increase to nearly 20 percent of the total group size per year. We had a lot of momentum, and most in our community had invited their friends to come on the retreat. Our community was relationally invested and praying for this. They had the trust (threshold #1) with the non-Christians, so they invited them to come and explore Jesus, saying, "Every thinking person owes it to themselves to form an adult opinion about Jesus. Come check out Jesus for yourself." This appealed to their curiosity (threshold #2), and a group of fifteen non-Christians joined our retreat.

Rather than designing a retreat that was all about information we designed the experience around the five thresholds: places to become curious, to become open to change, to ask questions and seek, etc. In fact, once we all arrived at the camp, we informed the fifteen non-Christians that there would be four "rules" in the track. One woman rolled her eyes and replied, "Yeah, yeah. I know your rules. No guns. No knives. No cussing. Same old, same old."

We simply smiled and responded with our newly minted five threshold-shaped rules. We said:

> Actually, our "rules" are pretty different from what you might expect. #1: Be curious. (Everyone has to ask one good question per session.) #2: Be open. (Everyone has to share one honest and real thing that is going on inside of you with the group.) #3: Grow. (Everyone has to take one thing you are learning here and put it into practice in your personal life.) #4: Risk. (Everyone here is going to take a few risks. We are going to try out what we learn during the retreat.)

John and I knew that the path to faith wasn't all about intellectual assent, so we tried to design an experience that would get at *trust* (lots of conversation, good food, fun games, and silliness), *curiosity* (spending long hours reading the Gospel of Mark all together), *openness* (following through on the rules that encouraged openness, risk, and engagement), *seeking* (providing a wide-open format where people's questions were encouraged to come out), and even *deciding* (toward the end of the retreat we built in an optional, non-coercive moment for decision).

How did we do that last one? We invited those who wanted to learn what it means to be a Christian to take a short hike with us up the local mountain to a large cross at a lookout. Half of the fifteen joined us for the adventure. Once there, we shared conversion stories of people who made decisions: the two thieves next to Jesus (Luke 23:39-43), the two people who sold all they had for the kingdom of God (Matthew 13:44-46), and the prodigal son (Luke 15:11-24). Then we said, "In Mark you have been learning what it means to 'repent and believe' in Jesus. In each of these three stories, someone 'repents and believes' in Jesus. Who would like to make today your day to come home to your heavenly Father?" (Keep in mind how much trust building, exploring, and processing led up to this moment.) What happened? A student named Eddie was ready for that invitation.

Eddie had been taking the Word in, growing in his application of it, and debriefing what he was experiencing throughout the week. (Remember the discipleship cycle? Hear–respond–debrief isn't just for Christians. God's Word is powerful to move all hearts!) God had been using his Word to soften Eddie's heart and move him toward Jesus. Up on the hill by the cross, Eddie took this moment as his moment and stepped forward. He bowed his head. He put out his hands in a receptive posture. As we prayed with him, he began to shake slightly as the Holy Spirit warmed him with the Father's loving embrace. (And we've already told you about the great things that happened from that point on!)

To be honest, we had never led a retreat like this. We had never intentionally thought about the five thresholds to generate the content of an entire retreat. But this time we applied them to the plan for the retreat, naturally following the discipleship cycle pattern. Note: we did not assume everyone would cross all five thresholds. But we structured the retreat so that if someone was ready to move from one threshold to the next, that part of their journey could be made as smoothly as possible.

Consider some of the elements we purposefully built into the program of the retreat to make space for wherever folks were.

Trust. We tried to build trust through our "unexpected rules"—like Jesus and his unexpected words—by hanging out at the campfire until midnight, sharing stories, and asking good questions. We played basketball in the afternoons. We had fun together. We told them personal stories and let them into our real lives. We helped them become a community.

Curiosity. We aroused curiosity by making "asking questions" one of the rules. We set that bar, inviting them to be curious every day. This was a habit and a value, something we came back to in every conversation. We stated it and then reinforced it, modeling and interpreting as we went.

Openness. From the beginning we asked everyone to embrace being open to new things and to grow. The students probably did not know what this meant at first, but as John and I practiced openness and as their peers shared transparently about personal struggles, fears, and barriers to faith, everyone became more open. We helped the community become open to change together.

Seeking. Not only were questions encouraged the whole time, but the optional hike up to the cross was a practical step to seek. They had to select it. It was not required. By making it optional, we gathered those who did want to seek for more.

Entering. Up at the lookout John summarized the week and the journey the group had gone through with Jesus and each other. In order to know if someone is ready to enter the kingdom, you have to ask. That's actually what's most helpful to people who are at threshold #5.

This is one example of how the insights from the five thresholds can be applied not only in our personal relationships but also in our programs and events. This can be a risky thing to do, of course. I remember our questions and fears as we tried this new approach: *When we study Scripture with non-Christians, what if God doesn't speak? Can God speak to curious people through Scripture the way he speaks to Christians? What if they don't like the rules? What if people leave the week and decide they are done with their journey of faith? What if no one moves beyond curiosity? What if the retreat dismantles the trust that has been cultivated?*

This is part of the joy and excitement of becoming more evangelistic: learning to expect God moments. As you'll recall, this is one of the habits of witnessing communities: they expect God to do something and program accordingly! But this isn't for retreats alone.

APPLYING THE FIVE THRESHOLDS TO A SERVICE TRIP

What if you planned service opportunities with the five thresholds in mind? In New England InterVarsity, their hearts have broken for New Orleans since Hurricane Katrina. By God's leading, they have made this a huge priority. Every March, they have taken over five hundred students to New Orleans to help with the rebuilding process. Even though the project was run by faith-based organizations, many students who would not call themselves Christians loved participating in such a meaningful service project. The leaders of this project saw the incredible opportunity to help these students take steps toward Jesus but saw few conversions. This was not for lack of trying. They had evening sessions based on favorite Jesus passages, followed by an invitation to faith on the last night. But there were few people ready to make that decision at the close, hence the few conversions.

I (Val) consulted with the program designers, Greg and Paul, and pitched the idea of applying the five thresholds to their service trip. I asked, "What if we intentionally changed the content and program aspects of the service project to mirror the journey we think and hope and pray the non-Christians are on? What if the five thresholds could be utilized as a planning framework for a service project?" They gave the program a threshold makeover.

How did they do it? They intentionally added trust-building components prior to the project, putting in community-building and relationship-building exercises at the meetings before the service project even began. They began to see those meetings not just for logistics and planning but as a time for the non-Christians to feel integrated into the community and for the Christians to begin to form friendships with them. The whole group got together a few times to do icebreakers, talk about what they hoped to get out of trip, and learn more about each other's backgrounds. This helped the community to build trust with their friends even before the long bus ride to New Orleans.

Prior to departure, they trained all the Christians going on the project in the five thresholds, equipping them with skills to understand the journey a non-Christian has, remembering their own story through the framework of the thresholds, and helping them know how to have conversations particularly to cultivate curiosity and help someone become open to change.

Once on the project, the leaders aligned each night of the evening content with the rest of the thresholds.

Sunday night they studied Jesus' cleansing of the temple in John 2. Jesus engages a broken world and acts differently than what people expect. They asked, "What about Jesus makes you curious?

What about how Jesus engages people and this world is worth paying attention to?"

Monday night they studied Luke 10 and contrasted the American dream with the Good Samaritan. They asked the question, "What if the way to our greatest joy isn't passing by the needs of people and the world but entering into these needs?" They discussed the limitations we have as humans to change the world and how a need for something larger than ourselves is a necessary factor for world change. They extended an invitation to be open to including God in their quest to be world changers.

Tuesday night they studied Mark 8 where Jesus asks, "Who do you say I am?" They shared the gospel and charged students to consider how they would answer Jesus' question to define where they were in relationship to Jesus.

Wednesday night they went out and had fun, leaving room for play but also for people to seek Jesus by praying and continuing to talk with each other about who Jesus was in Scripture, who Jesus was to them, and what it all meant.

Thursday night they studied Luke 19 and watched Zacchaeus choose Jesus and bless the world through this decision. They invited people to follow Jesus as the first step to being agents of healing and change in this broken world.

By the time the call to faith happened on the last night, the folks who had started the week at threshold #4 as seekers, as well as folks who had moved to threshold #4 during the week, were ready to respond and enter the kingdom. The number of people who made decisions to become Christians actually doubled the first year they made this curriculum shift. The fruit has been pretty dramatic over the course of three years, having significant impact on over six hundred people each year.

APPLYING THE FIVE THRESHOLDS TO SPIRITUAL FORMATION

Once we started to design retreats and events for non-Christians around the thresholds and saw the fruit, we encountered a new problem: How do we create content and experiences that challenge and equip both Christians and non-Christians simultaneously? (As your community moves from huddled to witnessing to a conversion community, you too may feel this tension.)

I (Doug) was intentionally trying to get better at this. So I embraced the challenge to plan a weekend singles retreat for both Christians and non-Christians around the theme, "Faking it: The Search for Love and Belonging." I started off Friday night telling an embarrassing story:

> When I was in fourth grade, I first discovered *Playboy* magazine. I was playing in the creek near my house, and I saw a treehouse. Once I climbed up into it, I discovered a box full of such magazines. I brought one home and hid it under my bed. Seemed like a good idea until my mom found it. How would your mom handle a situation like that? Not like Arlene Schaupp, I bet. She sat down with me on the sofa and said, "Let's read this interesting magazine together." Page by painful page she took me through that magazine. "My, what large breasts she has." "Well, that is an interesting pose." You get the picture. I never wanted to go through this torture again. That was the last time I brought home such reading material! How about you? What was your early exposure to sexually explicit conversation or material?

Everyone laughed and groaned. We were all on a level playing field. People were ready to tell their own funny stories from elementary school. We were becoming an honest community, having fun with a serious topic. They were bonding over my story and their own stories. My invitation that night was to be learners. To be honest. To tell stories. To ask God for something real in our lives.

The next morning we dug deeper into Jesus' interaction with the Samaritan woman. She asks Jesus a question, and he stokes her curiosity. I helped them surface their questions, either about God or about sexuality. Everyone filled out an anonymous three-by-five card with one important question they had. We passed them in and posted them on the walls. Everyone could walk around the room and see what everyone else was asking. Curiosity was contagious.

Openness followed. Jesus poked into the Samaritan woman's personal life. Why would Jesus ask the woman questions he knew might expose her? Instead of shaming her, he was offering her freedom. As I shared personally about God's healing in my life, I invited them to take a risk and open up to God their pain, shame, and fears.

That evening, before we invited people to consider becoming followers of Jesus, we opened up a time for prayer ministry. "If you want to invite God into a place of brokenness, please stand up for prayer." Many Christians and many not-yet-Christians stood. The Holy Spirit poured out in power over everyone. Tears flowed freely. It was a beautiful moment to recognize our common human need.

After the power of prayer ministry, standing up to respond seemed normal. When I invited people to become followers of Jesus, six made that decision.

Sunday morning we looked at the incredible impact of the Samaritan woman's story. She has a simple testimony: "Come see a man who told me everything I ever did." Every person had a story to tell leaving the conference. Meghan (who had made a decision to follow Jesus the night before) told her story the very next day. God used her story to trigger a movement of God the following week.

Christians and non-Christians loved the retreat equally. Almost everyone left deeply affected. Even the non-Christians who did not make faith commitments really enjoyed the weekend and got a lot out of it.

What happens inside of us as we introduce the five thresholds to our community and then apply them in relationships and programs and events? We are forced to think about the non-Christian journey in all we do. We get outside of ourselves. Our planning shifts away from us being at the center (*What do we want to offer them?*) and tilts toward them being central in our planning (*What do they need to help their spiritual journey?*). It is a powerful shift toward servant-hood, servant-planning, and servant-praying. We take up our towel, and we wash their feet at our events.

This will naturally begin to shift how we train leaders. We help our leaders cultivate trusting relationships with non-Christians. We help them identify with the confusion, thoughts, and emotions that non-Christians can go through as they risk to learn more about Jesus. We equip them with questions so that they can be guides (not experts) on faith. We help them be transparent about their own life with God, including the places of doubt, pain, and fear they have struggled with and may continue to struggle with. Ultimately we are cultivating the hearts of our leaders to see people the way Jesus saw the Samaritan woman.

Whether introducing an entire community to the five thresholds, beginning to apply the thresholds in individual relationships, or shaping our events and programs around them, we are doing an incredibly important thing: we are mobilizing relational evangelism. And this important macrostrategy goes a long way toward helping any community break the huddle and become a witnessing community. We've come to see that even the most stuck, fearful, satisfied huddled community can break the huddle and grow its witness in this way. Huddled communities, through nurturing discipleship momentum and mobilizing relational evangelism, really can become witnessing communities.

PRAYER

Father, we want to be a community where skeptics and seekers can safely explore faith and discover you for themselves. Move us out of our Christian huddle and into real relationships with people who do not yet know you. I believe that you are at work around me to seek and save the lost. Open my eyes so I can see the people you have put into my life, so that I can show them your love and point them toward your Son, Jesus. Equip me to help them on their spiritual journey.

[Listening Prayer] Father, please bring someone to mind now and help me pay attention to how you might be at work in them. (Pause and listen.) Show me how to be a friend to this person this week. Amen.

DISCUSSION

1. Which of the five thresholds are you personally most comfortable with and skilled in when it comes to walking with non-Christians? Which are you least skilled in?

2. How about your community? Which threshold is your community best at? Which threshold is most difficult for your community?

3. Write down the names of two of your friends or family members and try to discern which threshold they are in. Find a prayer partner to help you pray for them regularly.

4. Give an example of a conversation where you were trying to help someone cross from one threshold to the next. What did you say? When have you gotten stuck knowing how to help someone cross a threshold?

PART THREE

TWO MACRO-STRATEGIES FOR BECOMING A CONVERSION COMMUNITY

Huddled   Witnessing   Conversion

Nurture discipleship momentum   Embrace God movements

Mobilize relational evangelism   Align vision, structures, and people

6

EMBRACE GOD MOVEMENTS

On the final night of the New Orleans Katrina project, Adam left disappointed but with a plan. It was the night when they invited students to consider following Jesus, and Adam had felt sure there were students from the University of Rhode Island (URI) who were ready to make decisions to follow Jesus. Yet none of them had stood.

It had been an amazing week filled with incredible conversations. God was clearly at work in the room and there were wonderful God moments happening, but not specifically with the URI community. They seemed to be missing out. Adam went to bed expressing his disappointment to peers and to God in prayer. And that's when something happened. Adam had an immediate and clear sense in his gut: *Oh no . . . we're not done here. There are students who are ready to become Christians who did not stand.* He had a sense of urgency from the Holy Spirit that people were actually ready to make decisions. They had seen enough. They were ready.

So Adam felt prompted by God to offer each non-Christian a personal debrief and a second invitation to consider following Jesus on the twenty-four-hour bus ride home. He told his staff team and his student leaders about this prompting. Many of them were friends with these seekers, and Adam encouraged them to consider being a part of the on-the-road debrief and invitation to faith.

So very early the next morning when thirty students got on the bus for the ride back to Rhode Island, Adam prepared to help the non-Christian students debrief. Adam's questions were simple enough:

- What was your favorite part of the week?

- How did you experience God this week?

- How do you think God has been speaking to you this week?

- How do you want to respond to what God is saying?

Nick was the first person that Adam talked to. As they debriefed the week together, it was clear that something was still happening inside of Nick. He did not understand the gospel still, so they talked about it for a long time until it seemed that Nick understood. Adam was helping Nick clarify his quest, identify his questions and confusion, and move forward as a seeker. This is a great example of beautiful fourth threshold servanthood.

Then, when Adam asked Nick if he wanted to make a decision to follow Jesus, Nick said yes! What a God moment. After they prayed Adam told Nick, "This will be a moment you will remember for the rest of your life—on a bus, somewhere in the middle of the South, in the middle of the night, becoming a follower of Jesus!" A beautiful God moment, indeed. But that moment was not the end of the story.

First Adam cast vision with Nick, helping him realize that as a new Christian he now had a personal story to tell. So, just like the woman at the well, Nick returned to his seat and began to share his story immediately with his seeker friends. Then Adam texted all his friends on the bus with the news to encourage them as they too were having debrief and follow-up conversations with their non-Christian friends. As for Adam? He then fell asleep, content that God was at work, praying that his witnessing community would become a conversion community.

When Adam finally woke up his phone was exploding with text after text from his friends, each one updating him with more and more people who had made faith decisions while he was asleep. All in all, six students came to New Orleans who were merely curious or open, and a week later all six had made decisions to follow Jesus during that momentous bus ride home.

How did this happen? Only hours before, Adam had been frustrated by the lack of response among the students. And hours later there was a genuine movement of God happening. Not only were the Christians on the bus open to God moments, but they were also open to the possibility that those moments might become God movements. By embracing God movements, they were able to cooperate with this remarkable move of the Spirit on the bus.

What does it look like to embrace a God movement? Here's how it went down on that bus ride. Adam had experienced a God moment. God had responded to his discontented prayer with urgency, hope, and courage to have another conversation with the non-Christians on the trip. Rather than keep this to himself, Adam shared the God moment with others, which wound up helping his Christian community have similar faith and courage. God used Adam to catalyze something in his Christian friends. It turns out some of his friends (Zack, Lauren, and Justin, for example) had also gotten a little discouraged and confused about what God was doing on the trip. These three Christians were so frustrated that they honestly wanted to retreat, to commiserate in a huddle, to give up. That's how tired their hearts were. But by sharing with his friends, Adam made it possible for the whole group to embrace a real God movement—God encouraging and empowering all the Christians on the bus.

There was another God moment when Adam met with Nick on the bus ride home. God met Nick right on the bus and brought him home into his kingdom. Another great God moment. But instead of being content with that one moment, Adam encouraged Nick to share his story with others—stirring the thoughts and hearts of his non-Christian friends, opening the door to a potential God movement. By cooperating with what God was already doing, they were opening themselves up for a movement of God.

And that's exactly what happened: Zack, Lauren, and Justin (empowered and filled with hope by God) had debrief conversations with Katherine, Tessa, Taylor, Katie, and Emma (who were feeling thoughtful about their friend Nick's story). Good questions were asked, dots were connected, and there was more discernment within the non-Christians themselves about what God was doing. God used these debrief conversations to help open their eyes and help their souls yearn for a real relationship with himself. Individual God moments were adding momentum to the God movement on the bus. Each brand-new Christian would go back to their seat and "pull a woman at the well"—they would talk about their God moment and tell their story of new faith with their friends.

Interestingly, expectations among the non-Christians began to grow about what their own meeting with Adam, Zack, Lauren, or Justin would be like. The conversations among them became further debriefs: the non-Christian students grew more honest with each other, and layers of insight and understanding about God, themselves, and the community began to grow.

In many ways this is how most God movements tend to happen—multiple God moments blossom into a movement of God for the whole community. For example, when our friend Matthew Hemsley became a Christian in London in 1996, he was reborn into just such a dynamic. St. Paul's, Onslow Square, in the Church of England was where Matthew attended an Alpha course and became a Christian. In that church it was the norm for a God moment to become a God movement. Right after becoming a Christian he was asked to share his testimony from up front on a Sunday—the spark of his new faith was purposefully spread around to others. Also, it seemed totally natural to Matthew that God would want to do something *through* him in his workplace and in his circles and spheres of influence. *Of course* he invited friends to come to an Alpha course to learn about Jesus. *Of course* he decided to start making movies (his vocation) with Christian themes. God moments, in this way, *want* to become God movements.

So if you are leading a witnessing community but have a holy discontent for more, take great hope in this gospel reality: there is built-in momentum for witnessing communities to become conversion communities. God moments want to become God movements.

A COMMUNITY'S ABILITY TO EMBRACE GOD MOVEMENTS

But does that mean that all a leader of a witnessing church can do is simply have hope and wait for the God movement to blossom? Not at all, for two reasons. First, there is that pesky reality of evangelism entropy that we've already discussed: because of our fleshly temptations, the stratagems of our enemy, and huddled tendencies, there is also a constant backward push on any community's witness health. So real leadership is called for.

Second, for a witnessing community to become a conversion community (and actually sustain it over time) the community needs to actively embrace God movements (see figure 6.1). Every conversion community we've been with has had these God-authored, inspiring movements of the Spirit, but they have also actively embraced and welcomed those movements.

How does a whole community respond to a God moment in such a way that they are welcoming and embracing a God movement? We have only seen this happen through careful leadership—specifically, leadership that tends to three elements of the community: their vision, their structures, and their people. It may seem surprising that a community's spiritual embrace of a God movement is wrapped up in such seemingly mundane practical matters, but this is precisely what we have observed. How do you help a community embrace God movements? It is not enough to merely say loudly, "Hey, let's embrace God movements!"

Rather, in conversion communities vision, structures, and people are all shaped (whether purposefully or not) to make space for God moments to blossom into God movements. It seems to take all three elements of a community's culture for the community to fully embrace a God movement.

For example, we were moved to hear of the beautiful culture that existed at St. Paul's, Onslow Square, and the ways that our friend Matthew came to faith and grew in the faith. But how was that culture created? Through robust leadership that shaped the vision, the structures, and the people of the community. Matthew got to experience this powerful leadership firsthand.

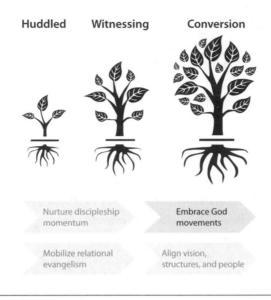

Figure 6.1. Embracing God movements

Matthew was eventually part of a group that was sent by St. Paul's to plant another church—St. Mary's, Bryanston Square. And this gave Matthew the opportunity not only to thrive in a conversion community but to peer behind the curtain to see what kind of leadership it took to create the culture. In fact, looking back, Matthew feels that the church's culture was what it was in large part because of the leader, John Peters.

What marked John's leadership? First, John paid attention to vision. He cast vision constantly, repeating key words and phrases all the time. For example, "Church is a place where everyone gets to play," and "There is something happening right now. So respond now." Twenty years later Matthew still remembers the phrases John would use to cast the vision, to create a culture where every God moment was seen as the start of something big.

John also paid attention to structures. New believers were always invited up on stage to give testimonies, and examples of God working through people were celebrated publicly. Alpha was a central structure with built-in places for people to serve and step up as believers—with very few inherent barriers in the leadership structures.

Because they had a simple, clear central program (Alpha), people didn't have to be clever or inventive to do evangelism.

Perhaps John's greatest gift as a leader, according to Matthew, was his ability to see gifts in people and invite them to use those gifts. "I see this in you" was a common refrain in John's ministry. As Matthew reflects, "John was always looking for people's gifts, recognizing those gifts, and saying: go! He was always watching and blessing any kind of gift he saw."[1]

Vision. Structures. People. What happened to this church plant that started with two hundred people and a strong culture of witness? Ten years later there were two thousand people at the church. (And this in a city and country where Christianity has been on a drastic decline for decades.)

There seems to be a connection between conversion communities and robust leadership that tends to vision, structures, and people. In fact, every conversion community we've worked with that has sustained for the long haul has had this same kind of robust leadership in play. We've come to call this robust approach to leadership that always touches vision, structures, and people the *leadership cycle*.

THE LEADERSHIP CYCLE: VISION–STRUCTURES–PEOPLE

The leadership cycle isn't a fancy new approach to leadership but is simply our way of describing this approach to leadership that is always careful to tend to three different areas that are a part of community-wide change: vision, structures, and people.

We (Doug and Val) have worked for four years, testing and improving this leadership insight and other community growth insights with student leaders on dozens of campuses across the country. We are grateful to InterVarsity Christian Fellowship for giving us the opportunity and honor of leading such a creative and innovative learning process. Like the discipleship cycle and the five thresholds, the leadership cycle came out of our long-distance learning community, with lots of trial and error. We kept trying to remove one of the three parts or see if we could add a fourth or fifth. And we kept returning to these three.[2]

You can see the dynamic of this threefold leadership approach in figure 6.2.

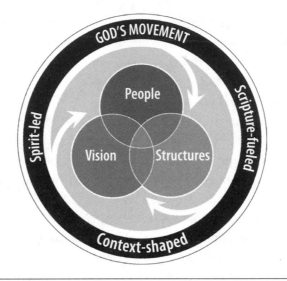

Figure 6.2. The leadership cycle

Vision–structures–people. In our experience, these three lenses combine together to make a reliable framework for leading communities and teams. We use the leadership cycle everywhere we go and serve, especially with communities that feel called to community-wide change. So, what exactly are these three areas of leadership?

Vision. Vision clarifies the change process. Vision might be a fresh word from God from the Scriptures that links deep into the heart of the movement leader. As the leader shares this vision, the community of God embraces it. It galvanizes the community toward mission. Vision looks ahead with hope—recognizing the current reality—by using words to describe a "preferred picture of the future," a compelling new reality that is worth giving our time, energy, and lives to in the name of Jesus. Vision is Jesus telling his disciples before his ascension, "You will be my witnesses." Vision is the Acts community agreeing with one mind that the apostles would devote themselves to prayer and to serving the Word.

Vision never gets old. You never graduate from vision. If you do, hearts drift and passion wanes. Life with God can become a routine and not a fresh encounter of the Spirit that fuels a desire to know God more every day. Without vision we may become apathetic. Evangelism may become rote or, worse, dreary. People may become projects. Conversions may become badges of honor "proving" our worth to God. We may become self-important. Vision is a key element in embracing God movements.

Structures. But vision has to be "incarnated," to be lived out in real time. Vision needs flesh. Structure is where the community gathers. Structure is how the amazing, life-giving community lives out its life together. That may sound strange, but we all gather somewhere, at some common time.

New visitors may not be able to describe it, but our structure and the culture of our community are the first things they experience about us. Our structure is how we live out our vision, our welcome in the name of Jesus. Wise leaders will understand this and find ways to think creatively about how to make our structure more in line with the vision God has given us. Our structures tend to have more influence on our values than we might think. We assume our values shape our structures, but the opposite is true as well.

Jesus' vision for the disciples was that they would be his witnesses, so how did that get lived out? First it was in Jesus' training school, his discipleship cohort and road trips all over the place, by doing ministry together and debriefing. Then the system needed to change after Jesus' ascension. The transition structure was gathering the 120 followers in devoted prayer. The prayer meeting was the structure, incubating them for what God would do next. After Pentecost they needed a whole new set of systems. The witnessing community was lived out in real life, in structures such as meeting in homes, temple gatherings for prayer, gathering for teaching, meals together, and sharing what people owned. When we say structure, we mean the Sunday morning service, leaders meeting, events, teams, organizational chart of employees, human resources department, training, and so on.

Some systems may be brand new, while others may be modifications of what already exists. Going to the temple already existed for Jesus' disciples, but it was infused with new meaning for the witnessing community. These small gatherings of new friends from all parts of the world in people's homes was a new structure.

We tend to have a love/hate relationship with talking about structures. Some people never want to discuss them or they dismiss them. Some talk about structures as if they are a god. It is true that fretting over structures can replace our confidence in God. In fact, some of the worst church arguments are about possible structural changes. It is tempting to think or to fear thinking that a structural change is the silver bullet for God's kingdom to arrive on earth as it is in heaven.

Structures can subtly be a bottleneck for vision and people growth. We cannot see the ways in which the systems that once were so life giving have become "old wineskins." They used to be new and vibrant. When we start neglecting to look carefully and wisely at our structures, we start neglecting people and vision.

People. People are the most important part of our communities. Although this is obvious, it has to be repeated again and again. It is all about the people. People, submitted to Jesus and anointed by his Spirit, are absolutely amazing. Revolutionary. Unstoppable. Remember Ryan back in our introduction? No one would have picked him to be a movement leader when he was twenty-two. No one except Jesus could have imagined what his life, submitted to God's purposes, would look like. What fruit, what love, what fire.

Jesus invested deeply in twelve. And in seventy. People. People who would slowly embrace his vision and values and live out his kingdom after the resurrection. People were Jesus' plan. Robert Coleman got it right in *The Master Plan of Evangelism*—the plan is the people.[3]

We too need to call out the best in people. We point out and develop their gifts. We release them, in the power of the Spirit, to live out their kingdom dreams. Communities that do a great job of developing their people are amazing places to thrive, places of great joy and fruit. We always need to be thinking about our people and their development in Christ. This never gets old. This never goes away. We never graduate to better ministry beyond our people. People last forever.

Vision–structures–people. It is striking to us that conversion communities call for this kind of leadership. Even the very first conversion community seems to have been led in just such a way. Consider the early church conversion community in Acts 6. The chapter begins with a structure problem: there is painful inequity in their mercy ministry structure. This systems glitch is the presenting issue that forces the town hall meeting. "Now in these days when the disciples were increasing in number, a complaint by the Hellenists arose against the Hebrews because their widows were being neglected in the daily distribution. And the twelve summoned the full number of the disciples" (Acts 6:1-2 ESV).

The Hellenists were born outside of Israel, but the Hebrews were native. Unfortunately, the insiders who were born in Israel were getting much better treatment than the outsiders born elsewhere. The bias in the system was breaking down the community. But instead of starting with a structure solution to their structure problem, they put on the vision lens first. They clarify their vision, which allows them to remind the community of their leadership priorities. Vision reminds them of God's call on their lives and roles. And it allows for unity amidst disagreement. The people embrace the overarching vision. "[The twelve] said, 'It is not right that we should give up preaching the word of God to serve tables. Therefore, brothers, pick out from among you seven men of good repute, full of the Spirit and of wisdom, whom we will appoint to this duty. But we will devote ourselves to prayer and to the ministry of the word.' And what they said pleased the whole gathering" (Acts 6:2-5 ESV).

This paves the way for the people lens. Once vision is clear, we can look for people. Lo and behold, God has prepared the way for an amazing people solution. A new generation of leaders is identified, honored, and anointed. "And they chose Stephen, a man full of faith and of the Holy Spirit, and Philip, and Prochorus, and

Nicanor, and Timon, and Parmenas, and Nicolaus, a proselyte of Antioch. These they set before the apostles, and they prayed and laid their hands on them" (Acts 6:5-6 ESV). Clarified vision flows seamlessly into the people lens. We can infer that this new generation of leaders addressed the systems gap, taking us back to the structural lens.

The leadership cycle continues, returning to vision. "And the word of God continued to increase, and the number of the disciples multiplied greatly in Jerusalem, and a great many of the priests became obedient to the faith" (Acts 6:7 ESV). The cycle continues, and the beautiful Christian community thrives even more.

THE LEADERSHIP CYCLE AND COMMUNITY-WIDE CHANGE

In one sense the leadership cycle seems like a great and healthy approach to leadership regardless of one's context. And that is probably right—vision and structures and people are all important elements to tend to as a leader. But we believe the leadership cycle is especially important as a macrostrategy for those wishing to take a witnessing community and see it transform into a conversion community.

The move from a moderately fruitful witnessing community to a mightily fruitful conversion community always seems to require robust leadership. The conversion communities we've seen that sustain as conversion communities all attend diligently to vision, structures, and people. There seems to be something especially significant about robust leadership and conversion communities.

Why is that? We don't know for sure, but we expect that the intensity of labor, the immense spiritual attack, and the temptations we all face make leadership all that more important. Think of the three habits of conversion communities. They

- linger in God moments,
- lift up their eyes on the fields, and
- labor in the harvest.

Each of these habits is, in a sense, unnatural or trying. It takes patience, prayerful attentiveness, and relational presence to linger in a God moment. It takes vision and energy not to collapse after the race you've just run with a new convert but instead to lift up your eyes and be thoughtful about who else in that person's orbit might be affected. It takes great energy, perseverance, and commitment to really labor in the harvest. As much as we pine for a fast-growing Acts 2 witnessing community, many of us might shrink from the kind of effort such a community would require from its leaders.

Perhaps this is why the leadership cycle is so crucial for conversion communities, or for communities that *want to be* conversion communities. But what does that actually look like in practice?

Consider how God used the leadership cycle to transform a small group of seven Latino students in the UCSD (University of California San Diego) community called LaFe.[4] They knew evangelism was important. They even had a mission statement that fueled them outward. But it wasn't really working. They were not seeing friends come to faith. They liked the five thresholds. They prayed for their skeptic friends. They practiced the discipleship cycle. But they wondered if they were missing something. So they asked for help from Dora, their mentor.

Dora began her leadership cycle with people. This group of seven Latino students were very gifted, but they did not know it. Dora saw that right away. She knew that if the seven people in the community began to see themselves as leaders and not just members of the community, things would begin to shift. Dora sees potential in people. She sees leadership gifts that are ready to emerge. And the flip side is that she sees the leadership bottleneck. Typically this is the first place Dora starts in the leadership cycle, which happened to be transformational for this community to move from witnessing to conversion. She knew people in the community needed to see themselves as influencers.

Then Dora turned to vision. She asked the small group, "What is your vision for your small group?" An innocent-sounding question. They replied, "To create a group to receive healing and justice in Jesus." These students really longed for Latino students to come to know Jesus in a transformative way. She heard their prayers and saw their own passion for Jesus. Their vision statement, although nice sounding, did not capture the true purpose she knew these students had for their community. In essence, their vision was not helping them move from a witnessing community to a conversion community. This was a vision gap.

So together they began to rethink what they really hoped this community would do and then tried to put language to it. A new, sharper vision emerged: "Bringing the healing, freedom, and justice of Jesus to every Latino student at UCSD." What is the difference between the two vision statements? By clarifying "every Latino student at UCSD," it became much more visceral and measurable and accountable. There was a much easier way to know if they were living out their vision fruitfully. Their community already existed, so they decided to shift from the phrase "create a group" to a more active phrase that might propel the group from witnessing to conversion: "bringing healing, freedom, and justice."

This vision statement (vision), coupled with how they were all beginning to see themselves as influencers (people), helped them rethink how they were structured (structures). Was only one of them qualified to lead the small group? What if five of them each tried to lead a small group? Each of the five made a list of the people they knew on campus whom they might invite to be part of the community (much like the prayer map exercise at the end of chapter one). They changed their leadership structure to line up with their new vision.

This group used all three parts of the leadership cycle: releasing people gifts, clarifying the purpose and mission with a new vision, and changing the structure from one group to five. By using all three lenses of the leadership cycle, they embarked on a dynamic change process and became open to God doing a breakthrough.

Previously, their group met every week in a secluded classroom, a room that had a maximum capacity of about eight people. They moved their weekly meeting into a public space where a great number of Latino people gathered, the Latino student union on campus (a structural change). They began to meet in the most public thoroughfare. Everyone would walk by and notice they were looking at Scripture or praying. It took a few weeks for them to get comfortable being so public about their faith.

Soon they began to print out many more copies of the Scripture passage they would be studying, along with discussion questions at the bottom of the page. They would offer a copy to everyone in the Latino union, saying, "This is what we are studying together over there, just in case you want to read along with us." At the end of the small group meeting, when they would close in prayer, they noticed that students throughout the union would cross themselves, participating from afar in their prayer. They built trust by the mere fact that they met on the turf where the secular students hung out.

Next they worked hard to craft intriguing questions that would hopefully draw the onlookers to want to explore Jesus. They picked passages like Luke 4 and asked, "Was Jesus a revolutionary?" They were provoking curiosity on purpose to engage those in the second threshold. They said things like, "Jesus would probably hang out with you guys if he were on this campus." Fifteen or twenty more Latino students started joining their lively discussions.

Typically they would start the discussion as one large group for twenty minutes. Then they would break off into four discussion groups so that each leader was responsible to gather and lead their respective group. Each of the four groups slowly grew to about ten members. They had to print out more passages and add even more leaders. More people joined. They became known throughout the Latino activist community. They got invited to help plan rallies and cultural events. People liked having them around.

They also started the practice of closing the Scripture study with an invitation to commit to following Jesus. And people said yes to Jesus! Each week new people were committing to Jesus for the first time. And each week those who had just made faith decisions shared their testimony. Faith was fresh and attractive. More friends invited more friends. A movement was unleashed.

Tanya (a key leader of the secular Latino club on campus, Mecha) thought God was irrelevant and indifferent. She often would sit at the front desk of the Latino center welcoming people to the building. Each week these newly empowered ministry leaders gave her a printed Bible study with their intriguing questions. She was disinterested at first. Her nominal faith background meant God was just for Sunday worship and he did not make a difference in the life struggle of her people or herself. But those questions at the bottom of the passage perplexed her. "Was Jesus a revolutionary?" She slowly grew curious. She started asking questions after the Bible study was over. She eventually joined the discussions.

Tanya was one of fifty-seven Latino students who made first-time decisions to follow Jesus during a ten-month period of growth. A year later (at the time of publishing) the vision is still being lived out: "Bringing the healing, freedom, and justice of Jesus to every Latino student at UCSD." They have seven small groups, all born out of their one small group. Each week ninety-seven members on average participate. And there are new faith decisions most weeks. It is a conversion community. A huddle of seven people has been transformed into a movement of ninety-seven, with over half new believers. It is a movement of God. It is good fruit. It is God's beautiful kingdom bearing fruit just like in Acts.

The story of the LaFe community provides a wonderful case study for how a leader's attention to vision, structures, and people can help a community move from witnessing to conversion. It's a great case study, but it's another thing entirely to turn to your own community and discern how exactly to implement the leadership cycle as a macrostrategy for community-wide change right where you are. That is the task we turn to next.

PRAYER

Father, give us hope that you are able to do far more than we see today. Help us to lift up our eyes and see the fields are indeed ripe for harvest. I confess that it is tempting for me to believe that the harvest is far from ripe. Give us eyes to see the potential in people, to see who they could become in Christ. We invite you to clarify our vision and increase our sense of kingdom urgency. We give you permission to move our structures. We submit all of our people to you and your leadership. We trust you with all that we have and all that we are. Amen.

DISCUSSION

1. What is the vision of your community? Of your small group?

2. What are your favorite structures? Why?

3. How does your community approach people development? Whom do you know who has underutilized potential?

4. Like the LaFe small group (prior to Dora's visit), have you ever been in a huddled small group? Describe the ways it was huddled.

5. Which part of the leadership cycle comes most naturally to you? Why? Which part is least natural for you? Why?

ALIGN VISION, STRUCTURES, AND PEOPLE

The LaFe story in chapter six is an inspiring picture of God at work. It shows how God can indeed transform a community from huddled to conversion in a relatively short amount of time. This prompts us to ask how we can grow in influencing our own community. Toward that end, let's imagine we are in the shoes of the seven people who were open to partnering with God in that adventure.

Not all seven of the leaders started out understanding how to lead every part of the leadership cycle. Even their mentor wasn't always a leader who naturally tended to vision, structures, and people. In the past, Dora used to focus almost exclusively on the people lens. *Just inspire and equip the saints to see their gifts and use them in ministry,* she thought. Then God taught her to combine people and vision. She loved to help her small group leaders clarify their vision and their mission fields, defined very specifically. We first visited her ministry five years ago. She was the only leader we had ever met who insisted that every small group identify a specific "people group" they were focused on and pray for them each week.

The reality is, we all need mentors. The LaFe community allowed Dora to mentor them in the leadership cycle. She passed that on to them because it had been passed on to her. And God has used important mentors to continue shaping and sharpening Dora's leadership as well.

I (Doug) have had the honor of coming alongside Dora at various points over the past decade. In one conversation about three years ago, I shared with her what Val and I had been learning as we tested out ministry ideas across the country. I said something like, "From what we are seeing elsewhere, I wonder if your ministry is currently stuck because of your structures. You have too few small group communities for people to participate in. I wonder if you would see growth if you doubled the number of small groups from thirty to sixty."

Dora bristled a little at the massive scope of change I flippantly tossed out there. As she later prayed about it, she felt God leading her to focus on growing her small group ministry. By God's grace, over the past three years, Dora has helped plant about thirty more small groups. Yes, thirty! In fact, she is far better at it than I am. I asked her to mentor me and my team in how she does it. Last year I brought twenty friends to spend a few days just sitting at her feet and learning how God uses her to lead these remarkable movements of conversion.

The LaFe leaders needed Dora's mentoring in order to experience a breakthrough in their vision and how they saw themselves in Christ. Dora needed our help to see her structures in a new light, which also helped her become stronger in this lens of the leadership cycle. I often pick up the phone and call Val for mentoring when I have a structure blind spot. Val asks great questions and helps me see new ways I can tweak structures to fulfill the vision.

We all need help growing and learning how to exercise more robust leadership. If the idea of moving your community from moderate fruit to a harvest of fruit stirs a hunger in you, but you don't know what to do as a leader, we suggest you implement the leadership cycle as a macrostrategy for community-wide change. Think through your macrovision and the vision of each small group. Look at your people and ask, Who is ready to be released into new ministry? Try on different systems solutions. Vision, structures, and people—these lenses can shape how your leaders think about the programs and activities they have for their community. Let's allow Dora to mentor us as we break down the leadership cycle into its three lenses so we can explore ways to tend to each area.

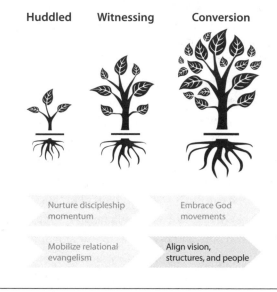

Huddled   **Witnessing**   **Conversion**

Nurture discipleship momentum

Embrace God movements

Mobilize relational evangelism

Align vision, structures, and people

Figure 7.1. Aligning vision, structures, and people

VISION

Vision is not static. Even though the LaFe community's initial work with their vision statement was important, the process of revisiting it forced them to clarify their vision and helped them uncover their very purpose for existence. They needed to move from a vague vision-in-a-box to a specific and compelling vision that would get them out of their rut and into a new way of living. One easy mistake with vision is to leave it at words alone—a collection of words that sound elegant, clever, and sticky; inspiration with no substance. The LaFe community had to move from important words into action steps so that they knew what to do. They started with this statement: *To create a group to receive healing and justice in Jesus.*

This sounds good and has words like "healing" and "justice" that are nice in a vision statement. But the leaders did not know what to do with it. Nor could they tell if they were making progress in it. The new vision statement was more specific: *Bringing the healing, freedom, and justice of Jesus to every Latino student at UCSD.*

A vision statement should be able to answer the question, "If we were successful, what would our community look like?" Can you sense the shift in the second vision statement? The phrase "every Latino student at UCSD" makes us want to start writing down people's names and praying for them. Changing the goal from "create a group" to "bringing" makes us look at ourselves and ask, "What are we actually bringing to them?" "How do we lead Bible studies that offer Jesus' healing and justice every week?" That was a game changer for them.

Your vision statement should help you know your end outcome. In this way, vision can help you set goals and concrete objectives that, if met, would tell you the vision is being accomplished. Setting the vision and goals begins to inform strategies for how to accomplish your outcomes. "Which strategies would be most effective to reach the vision and meet our goals?" "What are we currently doing that aligns with the vision and goals?" "What tools and tactics might we need to consider moving forward?" The vision should propel you to action. Underneath your vision statement you should be able to make a few goals that will help you know your vision is becoming a reality. In conversion communities, one clear outcome of the vision is that people make decisions to follow Jesus.

One of the benefits we have seen in huddled communities that launch an Alpha course is the way it forces a church to get more specific about evangelism. Almost every church has evangelism embedded somewhere in their mission statement or values. And for those who are already white-hot for witness, these vague nods to evangelism are enough to get them going. But for most people a vague vision for evangelism (for example, "sharing Christ's love with others") is so nonspecific that it is difficult to actually create change in the community. But churches that implement Alpha as a structure now have something tangible and specific to orient their vision and goals around. The vague "sharing Christ's love with others" can become a specific "inviting our friends and neighbors to explore Jesus through the Alpha course." And that specific vision can then lead to tangible goals, such as "every elder of the church takes the Alpha course this fall and then brings one non-Christian to the spring course." The difference isn't just about semantics and inspiration; it is about getting specific and tangible. A vague vision will rarely lead to community-wide change.

Consider a new church on the south coast of England. While it is very common for a church to have hospitality embedded in a vague way in its mission and vision (for example, "expressing Christ's love through hospitality"), this church got specific: *No one must come into our church without being offered a coffee and donut within the first three minutes they are here.*

Now that's specific! Again, a good vision paints a picture of what a community is going to be like. "Expressing Christ's love through hospitality" is too vague to paint a picture. But isn't it energizing to hear this church's statement? You can see it happening already. That's what specific vision does. This new church plant not only cast this vision but aligned their structures and people around the vision. The result? A huge hospitality culture! At the time of publication they haven't even been planted for a year and already they are averaging between six and seven hundred people in worship a week—many of them non-Christians. Specific vision matters in creating and sustaining a conversion community.

It is also important to *keep casting* vision for witness. Holy Trinity Brompton is another Anglican church in London. Holy Trinity Brompton (HTB) is the home of the Alpha course and is widely regarded as a model conversion community in a country where Christianity has long been in decline. In a city where many churches are closing and their buildings are being turned into bars and restaurants, HTB is now running ten worship services a week with a total of about 4,500 in attendance. It is known for being a vibrant conversion community and for planting other churches throughout England.

Mark Elsdon-Dew, who works at Holy Trinity Brompton in London and helps in their nationwide church planting efforts, reflects on just how important casting and recasting the vision is for keeping their community hot about witness. "Speaking is very important. It is very difficult to have a leader who can't speak, inspire, mobilize people. Leaders need to enthuse, speak the vision."[1] Mark reflects back on a season when Alpha was so successful and witness was so energetic that they decided they didn't need to spend the time in worship for three weeks in a row prior to a new Alpha course casting vision, announcing the course, and hearing testimonies as they always had previously. They felt they could relax on casting the vision because the culture was so red-hot for evangelism. The results were drastic—the numbers for the next course dipped significantly. Fewer people invited friends to come hear about Jesus. They learned their lesson and always cast vision ahead of a course now.

STRUCTURES

The LaFe community used to think the goal of structures should be to best serve the needs of the members of the community. Not anymore. Now they continually work with their structures in order to best serve the needs of those who are not yet involved in the conversion community.

Leaders who want to move from witnessing communities to conversion communities have a lot of work to do on their structures. It will take time—and trial and error. Members will probably resist. They like the old, comfortable way of doing things. Some people don't care if you fiddle with vision statements, but change one of their structures and you have their attention!

Here are some structure-related questions and possible answers:

- How might you make invitations to new faith in Jesus a normal part of more of your structures? Our upcoming sermon series on Jesus' love might be a great opportunity to try an invitation to faith after each sermon for all six weeks.

- What changes might you make to a few of your events to make them more welcoming to non-Christians? Let's make a list of all the words we use from up front that probably don't make any sense to a non-Christian and either find alternate words or ways of simply explaining them. (Check out the funny BuzzFeed video where non-Christians try to guess what our lingo means.)[2]

- How might you structure your leadership teams to develop people to be good spiritual friends well trained in the five thresholds? Let's take ten minutes at the start of every leadership meeting over the next six months to do some basic training on how people come to faith these days—including our meetings of elders, deacons, staff, teachers, small group leaders, etc.

- Are there ongoing events or programs that a core group in your church already go to that you could refresh as opportunities for invitation? This year don't just come to the Christmas concert but ask five neighbors to come with you!

- Do we have a place for non-Christians to hear the basics about Jesus and the Christian faith? Let's start an Alpha course and cast vision for how the congregation can use this structure as a tool in their own relational evangelism.

In a book on relational evangelism it might be tempting to think that structures are irrelevant. After all, we're arguing that holding evangelistic events, for example, will not automatically create community-wide change or alter your witness temperature. But there are important structures that can serve our relational evangelism. (Asking a friend, "Hey, want to come to a concert at my church with me?" can be easier to ask than "Hey, do you want me to explain the gospel to you?")

Likewise, different kinds of structures can be helpful for people at different places along their journey. If very few members of your congregation have trusting relationships with non-Christians, you probably don't want to bring in an evangelistic speaker. Who would come? You are probably better off hosting a fun barbecue where people can just mingle and get to know each other. On the other hand, if there are a number of non-Christians who've been around and are growing curious about the gospel, you might want to create a structure where they can explore the faith and hear some solid answers. In these ways and more, leaders should make sure their structures serve the people at each stage of their growth toward Jesus.

Matthew Hemsley as a new believer saw other new Christians up on stage talking about how God was using them already. The leaders of St. Paul's, Onslow Square, had created a structure (invitations to speak up front, space created within the worship service, coaching for new Christians in sharing their story clearly) that helped Matthew's God moment become a God movement. "This created an expectation in me: I am going to do something too."

At Holy Trinity Brompton the leaders are very strategic with their structures. Their Alpha courses are run with excellence, creating an experience for non-Christians that is quality and appropriate. As Mark Elsdon-Dew reflects, they are very careful with how a course is run because they want Christians to trust the structure so they know they can bring a friend. Teachers think through every word spoken on the course, and songs are chosen with great care. They want to avoid awkward, cringe-inducing songs or cliché words in a talk. As Mark puts it, "It is a safe place, by design." When they offer the courses, how many courses they offer—all their structures are carefully designed to reach their vision of witness. And the result? They have about 2,800 people a year go through an Alpha course, including the leaders and table hosts. Of course, God is the one drawing people to himself, but conversion communities are sustained when structures are tended to in service of relational evangelism.

At my (Don's) church there has been a recent emphasis on being externally focused. Vision has been cast, and people have even been mobilized to engage in relational evangelism. But we are still finding that our structures need to be brought into alignment with this externally focused vision. For example, for years Bonhomme has run a very successful Vacation Bible School program. A couple hundred children are blessed by this week-long ministry, and dozens and dozens of gifted people volunteer to pull off an excellent week of music and Bible lessons and games. Over the last few years my colleague Mary Oldfield (Bonhomme's director of children's ministry) has been making simple structural changes to the program that help bring it more in line with our desire to be more externally focused as a church. For example:

- Bonhomme reinserted Bring a Friend Day into the curriculum. The curriculum has always included such a day, but the church had never used it. Holding such a day would mean getting extra T-shirts, increasing the number of volunteer helpers, adjusting how many snacks, games, and so on are needed. Bring a Friend Day is costly on multiple levels. But by reinserting this day, Bonhomme's VBS has seen more non-Christian children come and hear the gospel—many of them bringing their parents back to the VBS showcase.

- Bonhomme moved the VBS celebration from Sunday morning to Thursday night. For many years we celebrated the successful week of VBS by having the children and volunteers wear their T-shirts the Sunday after and sing some of their songs in worship. This was always heartwarming for the congregation and fun for the children of the church, but Mary realized that none of the non-Bonhomme families—many of whom are non-Christians— were coming back on Sunday morning for the celebration. So Mary moved the celebration to the Thursday night, incorporated the gospel-sharing drama of the day into the celebration and included a warm welcome and trust-building moment with a pastor from the church. The result: almost all the children and their parents and even grandparents show up and enjoy the festivities. Non-Christians grow in trust toward this church they've never been in before. And they even hear the gospel expressed.

- The children and families are invited to participate in a collection for one of our children-oriented missions partners. Not only are the Bonhomme families reminded that we exist as a church to be externally focused, but our vision becomes tangible for the non-Christians in the room. This builds trust and even curiosity—*Why is this church so passionate about a small orphanage in Honduras?*

- Bonhomme keeps registration open. Because of the complex details that have to be arranged for all the children—items ordered, sufficient number of volunteers recruited and trained—we have historically closed VBS registration more than a month before VBS begins. But when Mary began to realize that non-Christians are more likely to wait until the last minute to sign up, she became unsettled with this structure. So, at great cost, Bonhomme has made the decision not to close registration. Children are even allowed to register and come on the last day of VBS! The other children's directors in the area have been shocked that Mary is doing this. But the result? Last summer over 70 percent of the families involved in VBS were not Bonhomme families.

These may sound like small details. However, this is the crucial (and often tedious) work of tweaking our structures so that they align with the vision and are much more fruitful in God's hands. The result is that relational witness is happening. Even though people resist changes, structures must be tended to and brought into alignment with a vision for evangelism if a witnessing community is to grow and become a conversion community.

PEOPLE

The people lens for a conversion community allows the vision and the structure to shape the development of everyone in the community. It is seeing the potential in people. This is what Dora helped the LaFe community to do. She imagined with them who could be in the room. She helped them look for the people who were not yet in the room and imagine how God could develop them.

Conversion communities place primary importance on the development and transformation of people. What does this look like? John Peters going up to people and naming gifts he sees in them. Holy Trinity Brompton looking for vision-casting leaders to head their church plants. Matthew being invited to consider how his moviemaking skills could be used for the kingdom.

In conversion communities there is a relentless effort to get people to use the gifts God gave them. Many churches that run Alpha courses end each one with an Alpha Celebration. People who are just ending a course are asked to invite friends and family to come celebrate the course and hear about the next session that will be starting in the next several weeks. Not only is everyone involved in witness before the course is even over, but often this is a time when folks are invited to help serve on the next course. Anyone can come and help (cooking, making coffee, doing dishes), and those with the gifts and temperament can be table leaders. In this way, mobilizing people is built into the very structure of the course.

Contrast this with the way that some churches tend to approach leadership development on more of an annual rhythm. Some of these annual rhythms can be rather intimidating and involved—including formal nominations and a vetting and voting process for mobilizing leaders. There is nothing wrong with such careful, ordered approaches to leadership development (Don's church, Bonhomme, uses such a process), but this cannot be the only mechanism for mobilizing people for ministry. (Bonhomme also recruits and mobilizes leaders through the Alpha courses on an ongoing basis.)

Witnessing communities are places marked by engaged, witnessing, trust-building, invitational people. And those people have to be inspired and equipped. Witnessing communities have strategic structures. And the right people with the right gifts have to be inspired and equipped to help create and lead those structures. Leaders of conversion communities must tend to people development.

FINE-TUNING THE LEADERSHIP CYCLE

Any community that tries to implement the leadership cycle will need to do some fine-tuning and adjusting to really reach a place of robust leadership. There are a few particular issues that leaders need to work through.

Leaders must understand their gifts and their context. Just like with the discipleship cycle, it doesn't matter where you start (with vision, structure, or people) as long as you eventually tend to all three elements and get all three aligned.

We know communities that started to create community-wide change by looking to the gifts of their head leaders. If a church has a senior pastor who's a gifted teacher, we've seen it work well to start the community-wide change toward more witness with vision. Use the word gifts of the teacher to ignite the change process, then follow up by aligning structures and people with the new vision. But if you have a leader who is more like John Peters, an inveterate developer of people, then start the change process with people. Then get the vision and structures aligned. We have seen other churches dial up their witness temperature by starting with a structure change—implementing the Alpha course, for example.

Deciding where to start doesn't just have to do with the leaders' gifts but can be determined by the church's culture or context as well. In a teaching-centered church, you might want to lead with biblically saturated vision. In a relationship-centered church, you might want to start with gathering key people. Do you have some strong structural ruts that are preventing true cultural change? You might need to lead with structure change in order to communicate how serious the vision is. For some folks words alone won't cut it.

Leaders must name and work on their blind spots. Every leader has gifts and weak spots. The trick is to be self-aware about where your gifts lie and sober and attentive to where your weak spots are. Dora helped lead her community to a different place in witness because she was willing to grow in her own leadership of vision and structures.

We all need help working on our blind spots. Doug always starts with the people lens. He cannot help himself. Val starts with the structure lens—it is just what her brain sees upon visiting a ministry. Don sees vision. None of these starting places is better or more godly than the other. But we all need help moving beyond our starting point to look wisely through the other two lenses. And this takes real effort and partnership, humility and collaboration.

Sometimes it is enough to name your blind spots and be careful to tend to them. At other times, leaders need to purposefully get people on their team who are strong where they themselves are weak and then really listen to those people. If you aren't great at casting vision, it doesn't necessarily follow that you have to somehow become a tremendous speaker. But it does mean you need to identify partners whom God has gifted with words. If you don't have a naturally tactical and strategic mind, it wouldn't hurt to read leadership books or lean into growth in that area, but you also might need to collaborate with folks who are gifted in evaluating, building, and correcting structures.

Leaders must avoid common pitfalls and temptations. What happens in witnessing communities if we do not look at all three lenses of the leadership cycle? We might get lucky and God does something extraordinary in spite of our inattentiveness to one of these areas. But more often than not we've seen communities hit a plateau in terms of their witness.

In our experience, one very common mistake is to cast vision but neither develop your people for the change you are inviting them into, nor change structures to live out that vision in helpful ways. Just casting vision is tempting because it *feels* like change is coming. Vision-casting can grab people's attention. It is sexy and exciting. Unfortunately, vision alone will not lead to community-wide change.

It is also common to change structures without a clarifying vision. This often leads to heated arguments and resentments. It is tempting to think that a structure change will alter everything because you are taking such practical (perhaps costly) steps. But if people aren't mobilized and if there's no clear vision for what the change is intended to do, community-wide change is rare.

Vision without developing people may leave folks inspired but unchanged. Vision without structures aligned to the vision may feel like false advertising. Structure without a vision to be a witnessing community may become static or routine. Structure that does not seek to develop people may feel more like a consumer community than a transformative community.

Developing people without vision may be confusing—there are endless ways for people to be developed, and without some clear parameters you may leave folks feeling frustrated and undeveloped in anything. Developing people without prayer and Scripture turns into psychology and self-help. Developing people disconnected from a community's structures may overtax them with meetings that don't serve the development you are hoping to achieve.

Leaders need to take care in avoiding some of these pitfalls, shortcuts, and temptations that they will definitely face while trying to create community-wide change.

Leaders must try out the leadership cycle in different areas. Consider some of the questions we are asked when we work with churches wanting to warm their witness temperature:

- Should we start a new service?

- Should we do something to connect with the hipsters in the neighborhood? Hmong community? Single moms? Muslims?

- Should we hire a full-time youth pastor instead of part-time?

- Should we change what we will do for Christmas or for Easter this year?

- Should we change the name of our church?

- Our head pastor retired. What kind of new head pastor will help us become a witnessing community?

- Should we change how we run our small groups? How we train our leaders? How we structure the fellowship time after the service?

Leaders can learn how to apply the leadership cycle to help answer any of these questions. By looking at the question through each lens (vision–structures–people) you can get a better sense of how to proceed. Let's take the first question as an example: *Should we start a Saturday evening service?*

First, put on your vision glasses:

- Why are you asking this question?

- What has God put on your heart?

- What is your vision for this potential service?

- What would success look like?

- How much time are you willing to invest for the sake of this vision? Five hours a week?

  Then, put on your people glasses:

- Please write down the names of twenty families who don't currently attend your church whom you might hope to invite to this Saturday evening service.

- Why are they not coming to your Sunday services now?

- Can you think of ten families who are members of your community who might join your vision and own it with you?

- Who are the gatekeepers who need to give their permission?

  Finally, get specific as to structures:

- Where will you cast vision to the whole community about this potential endeavor?

- When and how will you invite the above ten families who may become your partners to attend a vision-casting meeting to consider a Saturday evening service?

- How will you invite them to shape the potential Saturday evening service into an event they would love to invite their friends to?

- How can we use this Saturday night service to plant new small groups among new groups of friends who visit?

- How would a Saturday service affect other existing structures within the church (worship teams, communications, children's ministry, nursery, staff days off and rhythms, etc.)?

Using the leadership cycle to help you approach these important topics takes the conversation out of yes/no binary debates. And it helps people go deeper with God and search their hearts for how he is moving in and through us as we consider key topics. We are actually being developed by the Holy Spirit as we seek God for these questions. The leadership cycle takes us out of the presenting question, helps us grow in our kingdom vision, and helps us see who God is working in. Think back to Acts 6. Potential leaders like Philip were right there ready to lead, but the crisis opened the eyes of the community to give them acknowledged leadership roles.

THE MYSTERIOUS AND THE ORGANIC

When we first taught the five thresholds, we were careful to explain the tension between the mysterious and the organic. How does someone come to faith? Really, that's a mystery: God is moving in a bone-deep, unique way to draw them home. (Think of the farmer in the Mark 4 parable of the growing seed—the plant grows even while the farmer is sleeping. He just shakes his head in wonder at the growth!) Conversion is mysterious.

But on the other hand, as we listened to many stories of people coming to faith, we could see a pattern in everyone's journey. How does someone come to faith? Really, it's kind of organic: trust tends to come first, then curiosity, then openness. (Think of that same farmer in Mark 4. He watches as the plant grows, step by step, toward harvest. He's amazed by the growth of the plant but understands its growth and knows just when to get the sickle and harvest it.) Conversion is organic. It tends to progress in a certain way. Conversion is mysterious *and* organic, just as Jesus' parable suggests.

We believe the same dynamic is true with the leadership cycle. On the one hand, leaders who thought about vision–structures–people as they were leading their witnessing communities tended to have more fruit than leaders who relied on one or two lenses only. On the other hand, God is committed to his people and his church, and he will do whatever pleases him. When he brings revival, it is often despite us, and we will never be able to vision–structures–people our own way to revival.

Another fruit of using the leadership cycle is that you can pay more attention to God moments and how Jesus is inviting you to lift up your eyes and see what he is already doing. Each lens helps you look deeper into the harvest. As God graciously gives wisdom, you will learn to labor in the harvest and conversions will slowly become the new normal in your community.

Dora was having a God moment as she listened to the seven members of her Latino small group. As she lifted her eyes, she saw how God might use these seven in an Acts 6 kind of way and empower them to embrace their calling to become "fishers of people," joining Jesus in laboring in the harvest. As she cast vision to these seven members, they, in turn, had their own God moment—aware of how God might use them. As they lifted their eyes, they became aware of their Latino friends whom God loved. God began to call them to labor in the harvest with him to reach the Latino community.

The leadership cycle helped LaFe move from a witnessing community toward a conversion community. God used the community's leadership of vision–structures–people to partner with what he was already doing. God moments for Dora and the seven became a God movement. God poured out his grace on this community. All this Latino growth came through Dora, a Chinese-American woman. (Is that even possible?!)

Community-wide change is possible. This is great news, but change is hard. Managing change is tricky, which is why leaders must take care in how they shepherd people through a change process—the subject we turn to next.

PRAYER

Father, we are available to you today. We need your help to grow into the kind of community you long for us to become. You promise to give wisdom to those who pray for it. I pray for the leaders of our community: give them wisdom about our vision, adjusting our structures, and developing our people. Lord, please bring to mind people who are not yet in our community, people you want to love and transform. [Pause to listen.] Give me one way I can show your love to them this week. Amen.

DISCUSSION

1. Which of the three elements of the leadership cycle is your strength? How can you develop this strength and bless your community with it?

2. Which is your weakness? Who in your community is good at this lens? How can you let them mentor you?

3. What is one change (idea, question, or problem) that your community is currently considering? Try using the vision lens, the people lens, and the structure lens to reframe the conversation and see more sides of the change process.

4. How about your community's leadership team? Which of the three lenses is their strength, and which do they sometimes overlook?

PART FOUR

LEADERSHIP LESSONS

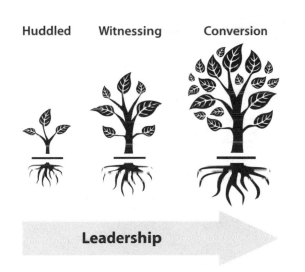

Huddled Witnessing Conversion

Leadership

8

LEADING YOUR COMMUNITY THROUGH CHANGE

When a community grows its witness, significant culture change is experienced. And change is something that many people resist. This means that those who are praying about and working toward community-wide change must be wise and purposeful in how they go about leading a change process for their community.

Even when you have clarity about what to do to help your church grow its witness, there is still the question of how to go about it. That's what leading a change process is all about. Many wonderful books (Christian and otherwise) have been written about change management, so we don't need to reproduce a comprehensive guide to leading a change process. But we have found it is important for people to have an overall sense of how to courageously move toward change. Toward that end, we have found a memorable image from one of Jesus' parables to be very helpful.

THE PARABLE OF THE FIG TREE

Let's consider again Jesus' parable in Luke 13 about the fruitless fig tree. Jesus is responding to people who are spiritually content with themselves and looking down their noses at others. To help them see that they themselves have a drastic need to repent, Jesus tells the parable of the fig tree:

> A man had a fig tree planted in his vineyard; and he came looking for fruit on it and found none. So he said to the gardener, "See here! For three years I have come looking for fruit on this fig tree, and still I find none. Cut it down! Why should it be wasting the soil?" He replied, "Sir, let it alone for one more year, until I dig around it and put manure on it. If it bears fruit next year, well and good; but if not, you can cut it down." (Luke 13:6-9 NRSV)

In chapter five we focused on the dilemma of the fruitless tree, but in this chapter we would like to consider the roles of the owner and the gardener in the parable. While we do not think that Jesus' parable is about leading community-wide change, we do find his image meant to spur on spiritual change to be striking, memorable, and helpful for those seeking to lead a change process. Consider three different actions that are involved:

- The owner pays attention to fruit—and is discontent when there isn't the kind of fruit there should be.

- The gardener holds out hope for the tree—and has a vision of what the tree could be like.

- The gardener has a plan to help the tree change—and is willing to dive into that messy work for the sake of the tree.

These three actions provide a wonderful overall picture (and basic three-step sequence) for how to lead a change process. While leading a change process, it is important to (1) examine fruit (and stoke godly discontent), (2) hold on to hope (and cast vision for a different future), and (3) have a plan (and dive into the messy work).

Examine fruit (and stoke godly discontent). The action in the parable starts with a vineyard owner who is interested in the fruit of his trees and is willing to examine the trees and tell the truth about what he sees there. He isn't satisfied with having a vague sense of the health of his vineyard, so he walks through the vineyard specifically looking for fruit.

When he sees something weird (no fruit for three whole years), he is not afraid to draw attention to it. He is not content with this lack of fruit, so he rouses his gardener to look at the tree and do something about it.

You may be a positional leader in your community with some level of discontent with your current status quo. Your desire to know more about creating community-wide change implies you are not satisfied. But it is not enough to be dissatisfied; it is also important to stoke this same kind of godly discontent within others. You do this by asking people to examine the fruit.

This is tricky to do, however. Ask questions about how many new Christians there are or how many conversions there were in the last year and people can get very uncomfortable. Some common responses are these:

- Ministry isn't about numbers; it's about people.

- Every single person is important.

- You never know what kinds of seeds we're planting that are being harvested elsewhere.

- Is it really possible to quantify spiritual change and rebirth in people?

- We are all called to be converted daily to God's will in our life.

These comments may be true, but they are often a way of dodging the hard work of examining the fruit. Is it difficult to quantify such things? Sure. Is it important? Yes. A congregation will not really change or be open to change if they are content with the status quo. And discontentment about witness comes from examining the fruit of witness. A variety of metrics can be examined to get at a sense of the fruit of witness at a church, depending on the church's context:

- How many people made a public decision to follow Jesus in a worship service?

- How many adult baptisms did we do last year?

- How many guests do we have coming to worship each week?
- How many non-Christians do small group leaders report are involved in each group?
- What's the attendance at seeker-oriented events (Alpha course, seeker worship service, topical lectures for the public)?
- How many new members did we add this last year, and how many of them were not from a church background?

No single metric is perfect. What is important is that you choose a couple of metrics, examine them honestly without sugarcoating, and face the facts. Part of leading a change process is helping to stoke discontent in others. At UCSD, examining conversion numbers created discontent in the leaders. Since then, Ryan has mentored many others in looking fearlessly at the fruit in their community and not avoiding the discomfort of the truth.

But what about those who don't pay enough attention to the fruit? There are a variety of reasons leaders avoid examining the fruit.

Dave was confident in his ministry philosophy, his strategy, and his general approach to ministry. He knew how to use structures to serve people and help them grow. He already knew the fruit was good in his ministry. "Who needs to study it? Just keep doing the same good things. People will be served and grow. We don't need to count. Goal setting puts all our confidence in human effort."

Sasha was a perfectionist, and she knew that about herself. She genuinely hoped and prayed passionately for more fruit. She and her leadership team did a great job of ministry at the first two thresholds. Non-Christians joined her community en masse. But they all got stuck at the third threshold, with very few conversions. Paying attention to the fruit would have been painful because things were not perfect. She wanted to avoid making her team feel uncomfortable, as well as herself, even though looking carefully at the fruit would have profoundly helped her team. They were stuck.

To Sasha and Dave, being told to pay closer attention to the fruit feels like being told, "You are a bad leader because you are not seeing more fruit." Instead, the response of courage and godly discontent should be, "Hey, God, this tree is supposed to bear more fruit. Give me the courage to really look. Open my eyes. What do you want to teach us?" If we could give them one practical suggestion, we would ask them to interview someone once a month—either a bright spot[1] or someone who has left their community—to listen carefully to what they are saying, and grow in understanding how people are actually experiencing what the community is offering. The discipline of creating a more robust feedback loop for yourself helps you pay attention.

Rather than creating a guilt trip or laying a heavy burden on a community, examining fruit and stoking discontent is really the first step in a process that is inspiring, humbling, and empowering. We have found that very few Christians (or whole communities of Christians) are motivated by guilt. This is why it is so important not to stop at examining the fruit and stoking discontent. It is equally important to marry that with hope and vision.

Hold on to hope (and cast vision for a different future). In Jesus' parable, the owner's discontent is met with the gardener's hope. It's fascinating how Jesus paints the story: the gardener doesn't try to dodge reality, and he doesn't try to make a case that the tree is really doing just fine.

Rather, the gardener faces the hard reality, yet holds onto hope that things can be better, that there is a future for this tree. The gardener is patient with the tree but in an urgent, honest, sober way. He knows the tree needs to change, and he holds out hope that change is possible.

Holding onto hope in this way is just as important as feeling the discontent. There is a definite tension between discontent and hope, but that tension is life giving. It leads to a sobered, inspired kind of leadership. This tension produces leaders who are not satisfied but don't give up. There is something electric about such leaders. It was Ryan's discontent and stubborn insistence that something different was possible that helped ignite the UCSD chapter for change.

It is then important for such leaders to help others be in the same tension. It's not enough to stoke discontent; leaders must also cast vision for a better future. The gardener in the parable speaks hopefully of the tree bearing fruit next year, casting a vision for a possible future. In shepherding a change process it is vitally important to help a congregation envision a hopeful picture of what's possible. This vision work is vital for creating change.

What happens if you don't live in the tension between godly discontent and hopefulness?

Roger is an elder in his church, where he has been a member for over thirty-five years. For years he's been frustrated with a lack of evangelistic fruit and hasn't been afraid to say so. But over time he has lost hope that things could ever be different. He has discontentment in spades, but communicates very little hope to those around him.

Mark is a moderately successful leader with great vision and grandiose ideas. When he preaches and shares his vision, though, it sounds idealistic and rather vague. His community is stuck at witnessing. He dreams out loud about having a conversion community, but does not express true discontentment with the status quo. He does not want to hear that he is part of the problem. And he thinks that expressing godly discontent is complaining at best or sinful at worst. He does not want to feel depressed, so he keeps focusing on dreams.

What we wish we could say to those who struggle with the tension between godly discontent and hope is that both are needed. In the kingdom of God, we do not try to iron out the tensions; we identify them, and wise leaders hold them in healthy juxtaposition to each other. Wise leaders also grow in self-awareness and can identify their own emotional barriers to being people of both hope and godly discontent. Which is easier for you?

Discontent and hope are not enough. In order to create community-wide change, leaders also need to have a plan, and be willing to get into the messy work of making it happen.

Have a plan (and dive into the messy work). In Jesus' parable, the gardener doesn't hold out an uninformed, vague hope. Rather, he has a step-by-step plan for how to move from the sobering present to the inspiring future. The parable describes a plan: (1) dig around the roots, (2) spread manure around the base, and (3) let this work for one year. There is a plan and, presumably, a gardener who is willing to do this hard, messy, smelly work.

What if you aren't willing to roll up your sleeves and dig around the tree?

Jane is a good leader and eager to grow. She loves leading her witnessing community and experiencing God movements. In addition, she can see the gaps and the places in the ministry that are holding them back from making progress toward the vision. However, she has a bias against rolling up her sleeves and digging around the tree. She has subconsciously decided that she has outgrown that kind of labor. *It is someone else's turn.* But she won't admit that to herself. Instead she quotes Scripture to back up her resistance: "'It is not right that we should neglect the word of God in order to wait on tables' (Acts 6:2 NRSV). We keep our head in the big picture."

Keith has done a good job of helping his community move from huddled to witnessing. He is a competent leader who has been in full-time ministry for several decades. Recently he has grown in godly discontent about the things holding them back. Although he is hopeful that things could change and he prays passionately for God to move in his ministry, he is still secretly hoping that the change will not require an overhaul to the current system he spent years perfecting. The old ways should still work.

Rick knew that the change process from witnessing to conversion would be hard. He was prepared to dig in the dirt for a week or a month but ran out of momentum nine months later. He wanted to get it right the first time and grew tired of the process of trial and error, reevaluating, and making adjustments. He had not counted the cost personally.

We told Jane that if she were willing to get her hands dirty, it would bring her out of the pulpit and back into the game in a way that would rekindle her love for people and God. She embraced the challenge, she changed some leadership habits, and her community has become a conversion community. She is filled with substantially more joy today.

We told Keith that what got him to this place in his ministry would not get him to the next level. He told us that he felt stupid not to have nailed this by his age. We said that if he were willing to learn some new things, his leadership would be developed and his influence multiplied for the next season of ministry he was in. He ate humble pie. He decided to grow. He told his peers the honest truth about being plateaued. He did not hide. Today he is a much better leader, and his journey has created space for his leaders to become learners together.

We told Rick that the trial and error cycle was a normal part of ministry and that it was hard to ever "arrive" and be done with our transformation as ministry leaders. We admitted this kind of role was not for everyone. Rick decided to switch careers.

The good news is our God is a God of change. Our Father sees us and our communities and isn't fooled by jargon and programs: he examines the fruit on our trees. We can have the courage to do the same with our Father, knowing that he does it in love.

At UCSD Ryan and the leaders of the fellowship made specific changes and called people to specific tasks in order to help the community change. Ryan himself was willing to change in ways he needed to—learning how to speak evangelistically and learning to partner with key leaders who had very different gifts from his.

We have seen churches and fellowships that stopped at casting a vision for more evangelism and then were puzzled why the fruit never really changed. If you are shepherding a change process, it's not enough to get people inspired by a hopeful picture of the future—you also need to suggest a plan for getting there. This doesn't mean the plan will be perfect and never need to be adjusted, but it does mean there is a tangible way forward and a willingness to dive into the hard work.

How do you lead a change process? Keep this image from Jesus' parable in mind, and you will have a portable, overarching picture: examine fruit (and stoke discontent), hold on to hope (and cast vision for a different future), and have a plan (and be willing to dive into the hard work).

LEADING CHANGE FOR THE LONG HAUL

Consider the change process that our friend Sam led. He has led his community this past decade as it went from witnessing to conversion, back to witnessing and back to conversion, several times over. Sam knows quite a bit about these crucial themes of discontent, paying attention, and digging around.

Ironically, when we interviewed Sam for this project, he felt disappointed with some of the fruit of his leadership and some of the ways his community was stuck in being a witnessing community. But we see something else in Sam. Here is how the past decade has gone. Decide for yourself.

Sam inherited a community that had tipped into a conversion community for a few years but then had reverted to a witnessing community. Like riding a bike up a hill, when you coast you do not stand still, you go backwards. As church leader Bill Hybels has famously observed, "Vision leaks." And in a conversion community vision can leak like water pouring through a colander.

Ten years ago there was a lot of evangelistic activity. There were special events designed for the curious, seeker-friendly worship services, and Christians engaging in conversations about Jesus with non-Christians. Evangelism had been at the heart of the community at one time, but now the word *evangelism* was no longer even spoken. In fact, Sam distinctly recalls, as he took leadership, he wrote a sermon about evangelism without ever using the E word. He knew that the E word would offend and alienate his audience.

Unlike Dave and Sasha, Sam was careful to examine the current fruit of the community, which moved him to godly discontent. It also led him to the leadership cycle to rethink what this community needed as its vision. Sam decided to anchor everything in one word: witnesses. *Every member a witness.* For Sam and his coleader Jerome this meant that every person who is part of the community has seen and experienced a God moment and can speak about that.

Eyewitnesses testify in court because they have seen something and have something to say about it. Sam believed that every person who was part of the community had or would have a God moment they could talk about with others. For him, *Every member a witness* was a message of hope he wanted his community to believe. This is the vision he began to cast. He began to pray and lead and inspire all hearts and minds toward this new vision. *Every member a witness.* Not just those with the gift of evangelism. Not just those who had an exciting conversion story. Everyone had a story to tell. God used this paradigm shift to move the tectonic plates of apathy within the community. The seeds of a revolution were planted.

Sam avoided the mistakes that Roger and Mark made by embracing the tension between reality and hope as he rallied the community around Isaiah 43:10. "You are my witnesses, says the LORD, and my servant whom I have chosen, so that you may know and believe me and understand that I am he" (NRSV). You will be my witnesses . . . why? So that *you* may know *me* more. Who wants to know the Lord more? Everyone. How does being a witness to his goodness and power help us know him more deeply? By putting words to how amazing God is, we see more of God's glory ourselves. This is the same thing that happened to the blind man in John 9. The more he talked about what Jesus did for him, the more his eyes opened to who Jesus really was. In this way Sam allowed God's Word to connect witness and discipleship in the minds and hearts of the community. The thought of missing out on God prompted the community to take their identity as witnesses more seriously.

There were two key parts to Sam's plan where he had to do some messy work. Like Jane and Keith, Sam chose to dig in. The first digging was thoughtfully and systematically reworking every facet of their weekly worship meetings so that everyone understood the new direction. Each week they gave an opportunity to respond, because they were becoming a community of response to God and his Word. The invitations to respond were specific and focused. First there was an invitation to new or renewed faith, inviting Christians and non-Christians to respond to Jesus by committing their lives to him. After that came a clear invitation to embrace the call to be a witness about Jesus in some concrete way.

The second area of messy work was facilitating crucial conversations with the small group leaders. Each leader was helped to think personally about what it meant for them to embrace their identity and calling as a witness. They were helped to go deep with God about this. Many hours of leaders' meetings were spent on the implications of being witnesses. How were leaders experiencing this vision? What were their questions or fears as their community was being led in this direction? How were the invitations at the weekly meetings forming a new culture of invitation and response in the community?

God started to grow this community's heart for people. Sam said that formerly the community didn't see deeply into people's lives, into what was really going on for them. Now God began to open eyes and hearts. They could catch glimpses into the brokenness or success and happiness. The community's mantra became, "What if God had something he wanted to say to people outside of the doors of our community?" Leaders began to believe that their community had something to offer others and helped them invite people they previously thought would not be interested in talking about spiritual things. As a result a whole new group of people whom the community had not reached before began coming and making decisions to follow Jesus.

This vision built momentum for the community. They began to look at all the week-to-week structures and ask, "How might we shape this around our vision of *every member a witness*?" This question led to changes in how leaders were trained—every leader was trained in the five thresholds so that at any time they could be part of someone's journey to decision and not wholly dependent on weekly worship.

Here is an overview of Sam's role in shepherding the community:

- *Examine fruit (and stoke godly discontent). Evangelism* is a bad word in our community, but it doesn't have to be that way.

- *Hold on to hope (and cast vision for a different future).* What if every person saw themselves as a witness? What if evangelism were for everyone?

- *Have a plan (and dive into the messy work).* Having invitations to respond at the weekly meeting is a total culture change. Create space for honest dialogue about how the leaders are feeling about these changes.

Here is an overview of Sam's work through the leadership cycle of Vision–Structures–People:

- *Vision*: "You are my witnesses" from Isaiah 43. *Every member a witness.*

- *People*: Creating space for leaders to understand and practice the vision. Inviting the whole community to be equipped and participate in the vision.

- *Structure*: Weekly community meeting with vision and equipping for "every member a witness."

Sam paid attention to how he shepherded his community through the leadership cycle. For five years there was tremendous growth and conversions in that community. The community is larger than it's ever been and has more conversions than ever.

So why is Sam questioning his leadership today? He wants more. He is examining the fruit and wonders if the community is satisfied with what they have seen God do. Sam is paying attention and allowing the discontentment to bubble to the surface again, believing that God will give vision and hope to what he is feeling and that he will once again get on his hands and knees and start digging.

EVERY PART OF A LEADER'S JOB

The image embedded in Jesus' parable is so helpful because it shows that the three parts of leading change are interwoven. The story wouldn't be the same if the owner had never walked around and examined the fruit. It would be the sad story of a tree sitting fruitless for years and years. Or if the gardener had not held on to hope but had shrugged sadly and cut down the tree, it would be a pretty sad story. Or if the gardener had begged for another year but done nothing during that time, it would have the same sad ending. The image is compelling because all three elements are interwoven into a single story and picture.

God has used this little parable to shape our hearts and minds as leaders and as disciples. We are honored to kneel with Jesus at the base of the tree and add manure and water and pray for fruit. When change comes slowly and you are tempted to become hopeless, remember this picture of Jesus, the Gardener, working to bring life and fruit and renewal to his beloved community. If you find yourself shepherding a community, know that you do not stand alone. You are doing everything with the Father, Son, and Holy Spirit.

PRAYER

Father, give me the courage to look honestly at the fruit of my life, and give me compassion as I look at the fruit in our community. Give me the diligence to roll up my sleeves and a servant's heart not to complain about the hard work. Give me hope that you have the power to transform us. Help me live in the tension between what could be and where we are today. Amen.

DISCUSSION

1. From the parable of the tree in Luke, what do you like about Jesus the gardener? Try to picture Jesus digging around the roots of your personal life or your community.

2. Which of the three facets (below) in the parable comes most naturally to you and why? Which area feels least natural for you and why?

   - examine fruit (and stoke godly discontent)

   - hold on to hope (and cast vision for a different future)

   - have a plan (and dive into the messy work)

3. What do you admire about Sam? What adjectives would you use to describe his character and his leadership? What is one way you would like to emulate him?

4. Think about a past experience you had leading change in a community. Write your story and share it with a mentor, asking for feedback as you grow as a change leader.

9

BE THE CHANGE

In the past, I (Val) led smaller communities through the process of transformation by helping our small groups become outward focused or by helping our leadership team become more missional. I assumed that these powerful experiences of success would translate to much broader movements of change. Then I found myself helping lead a multistate movement to help huddled communities become at least witnessing communities. I tried to inspire stuck leaders to overhaul their small, defensive, intimate, and declining communities. I had enormous amounts of godly discontent, along with some significant hope that the changes would be good and possible.

In 2009, I was asked to share at an annual gathering of an organization's senior leaders (about a hundred of them) some of the new things I was trying to help ministries get unstuck from being huddled communities. At that time I had some good ideas that were untested. A number of the huddled communities tried to implement these ideas. Their communities struggled as they tried to lead change around untested ideas. The leaders in these communities expressed frustration and critique for the ways my ideas were creating havoc in their ministries!

The critique was about the confusion of the change process, but it felt like the criticism was about me, my character, and my competence. Judgments were passed, wounds exposed. It was a difficult season. I toggled between feeling embarrassed and also realizing they had a good point but then feeling frustrated that the difficulties overshadowed the momentum to move toward witnessing communities and beyond. I struggled to listen to my critics without letting it define me.

Doug was a helpful partner in that season. He put concreteness to my vague ideas so we could test some things out. We were testing many things—too many—to help communities move from huddled to witnessing, or witnessing to conversion. Our lack of focus was overwhelming to the six communities that volunteered to help us. We burned them out introducing too many changes. We did not define clearly what we were testing, and since we were new at testing out ideas, it was difficult to predict what they would need from us to be successful. This was incredibly confusing to those six communities.

But we tried again. The next time around we knew a lot more about helping others lead change in their communities or, more accurately, what *not to do* in helping leading change. Previously we were satisfied with one or two leaders in a community embracing our action plan, but through failure we learned how important it is to build community-wide ownership in a way that honors people. Previously we had fifty ideas, and we did not know how to organize our ideas so that others could grasp them quickly. In this next round of testing, we boiled it down to three core practices, and people resonated with the three immediately. Fifteen campuses volunteered to test them out. By God's grace, the ministries grew by 26 percent over an eighteen-month stretch, and we saw communities genuinely grow their witness.

Breaking the Huddle is about hoping in God for change and then taking steps to help change the culture in our communities. We believe the insights, tools, and principles we've written about here are genuinely helpful for those who want to help their community grow in its witness. But there is one more hard-earned lesson about leading change that needs to be addressed: in the end it is we leaders who must be willing to be changed and, in a sense, *embody* the change we long for in our communities. In that sense, we go first.

Leaders who are humble, teachable, and malleable in God's hands are more likely to successfully lead change in others. We know this from personal experience.

GOD'S LEADERS WHO BECAME THE CHANGE

Consider some of the leaders God used to lead change among his people and how that process wound up changing those leaders.

Moses faced a difficult change process. He had to lead a slave nation out of bondage and slowly help them learn to put their trust in God. In order to lead them well, he needed to be a very different kind of person than the shepherd who once knelt before the burning bush.

Deborah was a wise judge, sitting under a tree, giving wisdom. Israel needed a military leader. She tried to recruit one, but that didn't go so well. So she switched gears and embraced the role of military leader, which is very different than sitting under a tree! The call of God on the people of God required that she embrace change for herself and how she viewed her role in leadership. God honored her and defeated the enemy.

Elijah experienced God in the fire from heaven as God glorified himself in front of scores of pagan priests who called upon a dead god. But God was not in the fire as Elijah hid in a cave. This time God was in a whisper. Elijah needed to know a different side of God and face a different side of his own frailty.

Jonah was supposed to help huddled Israel love their enemy. That was the last thing on his wish list, so he ran. God patiently pursued him, in the sea and in the desert, the whole time inviting Jonah to be transformed. We don't know if Jonah ever fully embraced the change that God invited him into.

Peter learned to love Samaritans as he walked with Jesus. But his huddled ways were not dead. He defaulted to them as he later led the movement of God. God needed to clearly get his attention and teach him to love Romans. God gave him a vision (Acts 10) to catapult him out of his huddled ways and into Cornelius's home.

The invitation from God is the same for us that it was for them. He doesn't just want to work through you to change your community;

he also wants to work in you to transform you. Will we embrace the invitation to be transformed, or will we resist?

In the end, we must all level with the reality that God's leaders do not just tell others to change. We need to embrace the change ourselves. We have the honor of being the first to repent, hope, love, and persevere. We get to model the change for our communities. And we embrace the new challenges and skills to make the journey wisely.

This familiar call to be the change will be tested anew in the crucible of leading a change process. For Moses, Deborah, Elijah, and others, leading the change process changed them. They were never the same afterward. The same will be true for us.

EMBRACING CHANGE AS LEADERS

How do we successfully embrace personal change as leaders? We want to suggest five paradigm shifts God invites us leaders into on the way toward becoming movement leaders.

1. A change in self-perception. There is a problem with success. It lulls you into thinking you have arrived and that *how* you arrived is what is still needed to maintain success. But that is the enemy of learning and growing. To learn and grow you have to focus on what you do not yet know but want to grow in. A fixed mindset says what I know today is what I need. A growth mindset says today is a new day to learn something new.

Two key barriers in ourselves have prevented us from having a growth mindset:

- Focusing only on getting it right—the right biblical passages, the right training, the right strategy, the right way to pray—versus creating space for yourself to try something new. The new thing you discover may not be exactly right, but it typically can lead you in the right direction.

- Binary thinking. I'm a success or I'm a loser. Either I win or I lose. I will pass or I will fail. A growth mindset thinks more developmentally: My strengths will become stronger, and I will eventually develop new skills in areas where I am weak today.

Please lean into a new way of thinking about your life and ministry. Please embrace the learner mindset. But count the cost. It is harder than it sounds to move from one mindset to the other.

Here are three things to consider to help you strengthen a learning mindset:

- Describe who you want to be as a leader in three years.

- Practically speaking, how do you want to be able to lead in three years that is different from today?

- What are some skills that you would like to have? Be specific.

Jane did this. Someone told Jane that people think she comes across as self-satisfied and impressed with her own ideas and thoughts about ministry. She does not communicate that she is a proactive learner. We asked her, "Is this the image that you want to project about yourself?" She took on the challenge, humbled herself, and embraced the change that God put before her. Two years later, the word on the street about her is totally different. She is known as a learner. She has embodied the change.

Keith did this. Keith was a doer but not really a learner. His leadership was plateaued by past successes. He was satisfied with what he knew. But then he ate humble pie and learned to lead different kinds of meetings. His meetings used be about delegating and reporting—what the team had been doing and what they needed to do that week. (Don't get us wrong—delegation and reporting are important, but they don't get you to conversion communities.) Keith embraced a learner mindset for him and his team. He would ask, "What is not working right now and why?" "What might God be saying to us in this?" "What do we want to try this week?" Keith said his people initially were very confused about this leadership shift and wondered if he needed to change jobs, which was painful. But eventually they saw the fruit of these conversations in their ministry, which silenced his critics. Three years later, Keith is a very different kind of leader. In fact, his team loves his learning meetings and they are growing toward becoming a conversion community.

Rick did not have the gas in the tank to change mindsets for himself. He could not embrace a learner mindset, which is why he wisely shifted roles. In some seasons of our lives we don't have the energy to change mindsets. It's helpful to recognize that and consider what it means to continue with the change you are leading. If you are unable to change your mindset, how can you ask others to change theirs?

If you are willing to see yourself as a work in progress, you will be much more malleable along the journey.

2. A change in mentors. Who have been the strongest influences in your life and leadership in the past decade? Who have been most helpful for how you think about evangelism and how you approach leading your community of faith? Most of us find a smattering of friends, teammates, mentors, books, theologians, professors, and relatives who shape our thinking.

As you change mindsets on your growth, it will also be important to widen the circle of the people you learn from. Dr. Bobby Clinton calls these various influences mentors in our lives. To become a witnessing community leader, you will need new mentors. If you imitate Ryan, Dora, or Sam from these pages, Bobby would say that they are now one of your "literary mentors."[1] Here are three steps you can take to get more mentors in your life:

1. Ask yourself whose leadership you admire. Who is someone about whom you think, *I wish I were like that*? Whose ministry makes you think, *I wish my ministry resembled theirs in this way*? Ask them to mentor you in a specific growth area. Take responsibility to schedule with them. Do reading and other assignments ahead of time. Try out what they suggest. Don't waste their time.

2. Create a resource document that lists websites, articles, and books that you want to read. Make a note of what made you add it to your resource list. Carve out learning days in your schedule—days that are specifically geared toward learning. Decide which resources from this list you will read and study

that day. (See appendix F, "Principles from Leadership Books," for a few suggestions.)

3. Sign up for webinars or conferences, and consider researching a certificate program or degree program that might help you develop some new skills.

Jane embraced a change in mentors. She went and learned from someone who knew more about leading conversion communities than she did. She has become someone who picks up the phone to ask for help when she is stuck. When she is writing a sermon or preparing a seminar on the topic of growing witnessing communities, she will even send her mentor a copy for edits and improvements. That is a vulnerable step to take, but she is growing as a leader because of it. And her community is in a better place because she has "become the change" that she hopes for God to do in her community.

Our friend Mark has now become aware that his idealism is actually capping his leadership. His idealism makes him come across as a little out of touch and is a barrier to some people wanting to follow him. Recently, he has gone out of his way to get some new mentors. After seeing his idealistic visions struggle to become realities, he has found people who are more successful at seeing their dreams come to fruition.

Then there's our friend Sasha, who has been plateaued in her influence because of her perfectionism. After seeing her ministry mostly get stuck and never make it to conversion community, Sasha realized some of the gaps in her leadership. What kind of mentor would she look to? She took a very different route. She hired a firecracker of a leader who knows more than she does about leading witnessing and conversion communities. Sasha listens well to this younger, opinionated leader and even allows the younger leader to mentor her. The age gap is not a barrier for Sasha's learning. It can be uncomfortable when the younger leader points out what is not perfect about the current situation, but the fruit from this choice has been amazing. Sometimes hiring someone who has strong godly discontent can bear fruit as well.

We (Val and Doug) got mentored in training, which is very important to us. We used to think good training was our opportunity to download all the information we had about a subject. We knew enough to make it interesting by telling personal stories and giving people a chance to interact with what we were saying. In hindsight, it's fair to say our definition of training was more like a big content dump than it was about training people to effectively live out the skill we were trying to impart. We found an excellent training mentor, Kim, who was also our friend. Kim would ask us a series of very troubling questions about every training we were creating (and now we ask those same troubling questions when others ask us for input on their training curriculums). "What is the goal of your training? In six months, what do you want to be true of the people who attend this training?" These two questions have transformed how we plan our training sessions. We think everyone who wants to lead a conversion community would be wise to let these two questions transform how they train or teach.

3. *A change in how we learn.* The three of us have always been learners. But learning how to lead our communities to grow their witness has meant a whole new level of being incredibly intentional about learning, reflecting, asking for help, experimenting, failing, trying new things, and rejoicing in the breakthroughs. Because we have been "all in" on being learners, we have drawn from all kinds of friends and colleagues to help us with the learning. We refer to this as creating a learning community or leading a learning process.

One crucial ingredient in creating a learning community is that we are self-conscious in embarking on a journey of discovery in which we all learn new things. It is not as if we three secretly knew all the insights covered in this book ten years ago. Not at all! You cannot lead a genuine learning community if you are not willing to be a learner and a leader at the same time. In addition, today's best answers and ideas are not good enough. You cannot be very impressed with your current set of assumptions about how communities grow and change. Our confidence is that our generous God will give us more wisdom than we have today as we move into the unknown together as trailblazers. Community makes us better. And a learning community means we learn at an exponential rate rather than just learning in our own little bubble.

When we lead communities into learning, we state up front, "For the next hour, this is a learning community. We are not going to do anything productive for an hour. We are just going to dig into what we have tried and experimented with for the past month and see if any new insights emerge." Leading learning means we state up front what we have yet to learn. (See appendix G, "How to Lead a Learning Community," for a template for leading a learning community conversation.)

Learning also involves testing. In the past five years, God has transformed how we rigorously test out our new ideas. As Val shared above, we never used to test our ideas.

My (Doug's) wife, Sandy, often asks me, "Do you know that, or do you just think that?" We have adopted Sandy's now-famous question as one of our mantras: Do we know this yet, or do we just think this? Have we seen it in a real ministry setting? Where? When? Who did it? How did it turn out? If we cannot tell the real story of where an idea took root, we force ourselves to say, "This is my current best thinking on this, but it is untested." This rigor has also forced us to have to consider our underlying bias and assumptions: "Why do I think that?" "Where did I get this notion?"

We had an "aha!" moment reading Jim Collins's *Great by Choice*.[2] He told us to "fire bullets first, and then calibrate cannonballs." In this centuries-old metaphor of calibrated cannonballs, such ammunition was large and high-risk and often missed the other boat. Instead of firing round after round of expensive and precious cannonballs, bullets were fired to test wind speed, the speed of the opposing boat and so on. Once you "pinged" against the hull of the other boat with a bullet, you could calibrate your expensive ammunition with great confidence and great results. Uncalibrated cannonballs are large, high-risk ideas that you hope will work but you don't know, yet you launch them anyway. We had been testing prior to reading Collins, but we adopted his language in our meetings. "Let's fire a few bullets on this idea and wait before we ask everyone to try it. Once it bears fruit and we know it works, then we launch calibrated cannonballs with everyone." By God's grace, today we fire far fewer wasted, uncalibrated cannonballs, though we confess we are still guilty of that at times.

A key posture for a learning community is to examine our assumptions. Some questions that can help with that include these:

- In the past, how did we think about this kind of ministry? What do we think today?

- Why and how did our thinking change?

- If we could turn back the clock twelve months, what would we do differently?

- How do we test out this new theory?

Emotions can be high as people process their experiences—exuberance at seeing fruit; regrets about poor decisions or dropping the ball in some way; or fear of failure, being exposed, or even being rejected. Some fear that they or their communities will never change. The learning mode requires honesty and safety to explore feelings while looking at the facts. You could come up with the right things to test or do moving forward from a learning community time, but if you have not helped your learners process whether they are ready to try again, they are likely not going to be able to start over. Here are some questions that might help you do this:

- What are some examples of barriers you ran into, places of failure or frustration?

- Let's look at both sides of the coin. Where is this working? Where did it not work? What can we learn from both types of stories?

- What are some specific questions we need to be asking the next three months?

- What clarity do you need from here? What do you want to be testing from this point forward?

- What do you want to do this week in response to this conversation?

4. A change in practice of partnership. Strong and dynamic partnerships are crucial to helping a community grow its witness. Community-wide change is not a one-man show.

Let's revisit Ryan's story from the introduction. Ryan is gifted by God as a visionary leader and evangelist, and he used these gifts faithfully. But he could not lead the complex change process by himself. Along with Ramiro, Megan, and Serene, they led a pocket of their community to become a conversion community, while the rest remained largely huddled. God saw the problem and brought a key partner for Ryan: James.

When James joined the team, it was clear he shared some of these same gifts, but he was also a pastor who was a strategist and skillful with difficult processes. James was excellent at improving systems, putting the right people into the right roles, and discerning how to work with structures. James needed Ryan. Ryan needed James. After James joined the team the vision of the fellowship didn't change, but increasingly the structures of the fellowship and the mobilization of people (and their God-given gifts) were brought into alignment with the vision. They began to see growth, and growth brought a whole new set of problems: How would they do follow-up with all the new believers? How did small groups fit in? How would the student leaders need to be trained differently? Piece by piece, structure by structure, they renovated each part of the ministry to work in synergy together.

Since those shifts, the UCSD fellowship has averaged one hundred conversions a year, even topping two hundred in several years. Recently they saw forty-five students become Christians at their very first meeting of the year! Real, sustainable, community-wide change has taken place in this Christian community. While none of these would have happened without God's Spirit moving, it is clear in retrospect how pivotal this powerful bond of brotherhood was to the process of transformation. Ryan and James repeatedly argued, hurt each other's feelings, came back and reconciled, prayed together, and then led together in unity.

Certified coaches are an amazing resource, but we believe that we can be amazing coaching resources to each other as well. Peer coaching relationships are either catalyzed when you identify and prioritize a key growth area for yourself or when you see a notable strength in a friend or colleague and ask them to use that strength to help you grow. Everyone has gaps in their lives. An important question is, Are we willing to admit the gaps in ourselves? And even more crucial, Are we willing to ask for help to grow?

Once we swallow our pride and open our eyes to the possibilities of peer coaching, the resources that God has made available grow a hundredfold. We don't need an expert coach to help us grow. We just need a peer who is willing to invest in us for a period of time and help us take practical steps to hone and sharpen powerful God-given strengths. This can be life changing for the person on the receiving end and remarkably empowering for the peer coach who is helping out. We love these kinds of partnerships, and we would not be the leaders we are today if we had not repeatedly humbled ourselves and received help from incredible kingdom peers.

The book *Canoeing the Mountains* offers a compelling image for leaders.[3] Author Tod Bolsinger uses the story of Lewis and Clark to describe the journey he believes all leaders go on. Lewis and Clark were commissioned by Thomas Jefferson to go explore the West. They started in a canoe until they were befuddled by a massive mountain range. Their assumption was that they would be able to canoe all the way to the Pacific Ocean. But the Rocky Mountains stood in their way, and they had to shift from seeing themselves as canoers to mountain hikers.

So they decided to leave behind the canoe that represented the plan for their journey. Bolsinger uses this image for what it means to be an adaptive leader. At some point in every leadership journey, what you once knew and relied on must be left behind, in part, to both grow your own leadership and help your community grow to a new place. He describes this process as becoming a more adaptive leader, which he and others would say is essential to leadership today. We agree. And every time we practice learning community, it feels like we are leaving behind our canoes.

5. *A shift in how you experience God-with-us.* Sometimes God is your only friend. No partner, spouse, mentor, or friend can understand the pain of leading change. At the end of the day, learning to lean into God is our only hope for peace and joy. We need his perspective—not more data to back up our case, not someone else who can tell us we are right or empathize with us. Not another book to learn what we already know. Not TV or a bed to escape into another world. We need God himself. Here's how each of us has shifted in how we experience God-with-us.

I (Val) have learned to process the messiness of life with God differently. In the past, I would look for who was going to take the blame for the current jumbled circumstances or feelings that often arise in the midst of leading a change process—the "whose fault is it" game. Today, I engage with God via intentional journaling. I call it writing out six versions of the story. I make myself write out as many narratives of the same conflict as I can. In the first few, I am the protagonist and some other leader is clearly at fault. In a later version, I am the villain, and it's all my fault. Then it is time to put God on the hot seat: it is all God's fault. Another version is the spiritual formation story, the ways God is using this experience to form me. Another version is imagining how a close friend would tell the story. There is typically an element of truth in each of these five versions. The sixth version is one that tries to accurately tell the story, typically trying to include pieces of all the versions. The sixth version helps me lean into my own learning lessons, proclaiming truth about God and his goodness while being honest about how I need God to heal, salve the wounds, and have mercy on me. The sixth version extends grace and mercy to others, giving them the benefit of the doubt and remembering "they're doing the best they can."[4] This version allows me to hold in tension many views of the story. What is the invitation from God in the midst of the tension? God is present. God-with-us, God-with-me. I have learned to rely on this promise, to allow God to be a friend to me in those situations. As always, sin is lurking at the door. Sins of anger, self-hatred, wrath, hopelessness, and self-pity still lurk at the door, but I am learning to recognize those dark places for what they are and turn away.

I (Doug) have always liked brainstorms. In the past, all decent ministry ideas that popped into my head felt like they were probably from God and should be acted upon. Some people loved this about me, yet it drove others crazy. I did not prioritize the new ideas, and people on my team felt compelled to do them all because I made them sound urgent and important. Some good failure in the past six years has led me to no longer believe that all the new ideas that pop into my head are from God. In fact, upon launching a new ministry effort today, instead of "This is a great idea," those around me hear me saying, "I have no clarity if God is in this idea or if he has something else for us. Let's keep brainstorming."

I never knew I should test my ideas. It honestly never even occurred to me. I just liked my ideas and then would get my team to do them. Some failed and some succeeded. Today I love to test ideas and see if God is in any of them. I try little pilot projects and study the data. What worked and what didn't? Why? I experience great freedom and intimacy with God in these moments. "I know that I don't know what God is doing right now. But I know he is here. And I know that he will reveal himself to us as we go." Ah, the joy of learning!

I (Don) have always been a poet and communicator at heart. But fears and temptations in life have made me want to hide away from the messy world. Being called into ministry to messy people has led to certain patterns in my life: a tendency to settle for less fruit as a leader when God might want more fruit; a tendency to be satisfied if things are "well articulated," not questioning whether enough has been said or whether real change has happened because of what has been said; a tendency to manage rather than lead.

My engagement with the five thresholds not only led to cowriting *I Once Was Lost* with Doug, but it stoked discontentment within me for settling. Doug's relentless revolutionary drive and Val's dogged pursuit of implementation and creating whole-community change have had a way of shaking my shoulders, rousing me from my temptation to fall asleep in ministry and settle.

As a result, this introvert who would just as soon hole up in a cabin in the woods somewhere finds himself not only knee-deep in the wonderful mess and beauty of ministry in a two-hundred-year-old Presbyterian church but also traveling to other churches and denominations and ministries to stoke the fires of change and give testimony that God can use *anyone* to be a witness. *Breaking the Huddle* is a project that, itself, has roused me. Instead of working on a zombie trilogy I have dreamed up, I am leaning into this messy research/book project with Doug and Val. A deep desire to be *useful* to God is starting to take root in my heart, right next to the deep desire to be safe and comfortable. And this new desire changes things for me.

It seems to us, in the end, that leading change changes you. If you hope to lead change in others, you must be open to change in yourself. This may mean a new mindset, new mentors, new ways of learning, new partnerships, and a new posture in your relationship with Jesus. But whatever it means, it is unaccountably worth it. And our sincere hope is that this book has involved you in a conversation that will leave you as changed as it has left us.

Leading change gives us an opportunity to know God in new ways by giving us experiences—living parables, if you will. Over time may we all become more aware of the invitations from God in the midst of messy ministry tensions and failures.

PRAYER

Father, I like feeling comfortable. I don't like looking at the gaps in my life and ministry. I am afraid that if I ask for help, people will see even more what is less than ideal about me. I invite you into my fears. I invite you to give me courage to see myself more accurately and yet not judge myself. You do not condemn me; help me not to self-condemn. Please give me one practical way I can become the change that I so desperately want to see in my community. Amen.

DISCUSSION

How have you changed as a leader since starting w/ Stonecroft?

1. What inspires you about the stories of personal change in this chapter? Which story did you resonate with the most? Why?

2. Pick one of the five areas of change to prioritize in your personal growth: change in your self-perception, your mentors, how you learn, how you partner, or how you experience God-with-us. Why did you pick that one? What is one step you can take in that direction this week?

3. Peer mentors are available to all of us, but we have to ask for help. Think of one peer you could ask to help you take one step in the above growth area.

CONCLUSION

Great Joy in the Work

Our involvement in the ongoing conversation about witness today has changed us, confused us, inspired us, informed us, and led us to what we think are some very helpful observations. These observations about witnessing communities and how they grow are summarized in figure C.1.

Huddled	**Witnessing**	**Conversion**

Limited witness	*Engaged in witness*	*Aligned around witness*
• witness is a concept	• witness is a value	• witness shapes everything
• non-Christian presence in community is rare	• some non-Christians are involved in community	• many non-Christians involved in community
• conversions are rare	• multiple conversions annually	• multiple conversions monthly

> Nurture discipleship momentum

> Embrace God movements

> Mobilize relational evangelism

> Align vision, structures, and people

Figure C.1. Summary of witnessing communities and how they grow

This diagram raises two important questions: *Where is my own community in its witness?* and *What steps can we take to grow in our witness?*

These are strategic questions, and much of our work in *Breaking the Huddle* has been geared toward helping people ask (and answer!) them. But above and beyond these questions, this whole conversation prompts a pulsing, overarching spiritual question: *Do I believe that God can actually use someone like me to be part of a God movement?*

We three believe to our core that God can use anyone to be part of a God movement. We have seen firsthand the most unlikely friends become amazing movement leaders. It is a joyful transformation to behold. Frankly, that is why we spent a year and a half writing this book. We believe in God's work in and through the most common people.

But sometimes all these diagrams can feel heavy and complicated. All this talk of growing a community's witness can feel like being asked to roll a heavy stone up a steep hill. However, Jesus claimed, "My yoke is easy and my burden is light" (Matthew 11:30). This doesn't mean that ministry and leadership and living out the kingdom and shepherding God's people aren't messy and hard and challenging and frustrating—they are all of those things! But they are never meant to be heavy.

In our experience, laboring in God's kingdom begins to feel heavy when we lose sight of Scripture's very clear teaching that God is at work in the world around us. He is seeking after the lost. He is calling people into his embrace. When we realize (and believe and trust) that God is the one at work, all our labors cease to feel as heavy. In fact, it is the joy of the Lord that is our strength (Nehemiah 8:10). Joy will be our crown. And it needs to be our daily choice when change is slow and our community is not perfect.

We end this book with a final, personal, spiritual question: *Do you believe God is at work today?*

If so, that changes everything. We aren't trying to roll heavy rocks up a hill. We are partnering with what God is doing. We are players on his kingdom team, a team that is inexorably advancing the kingdom forward. This is the joyful chorus of the book of Acts: in spite of internal and external obstacles, the gospel moves forward. The last word of the book of Acts is the note meant to be ringing in the ears of the church: *unhindered.* God's kingdom cannot be stopped. It goes forward unhindered.

PRAYER

Thank you, Jesus, that your gospel cannot be stopped. Thank you that you use an imperfect disciple like me to be your witness. Thank you for your Holy Spirit who equips us to do all that you call us to do. Amen.

ACKNOWLEDGMENTS

It took a village to get this book to print. Our friends and communities have been outstanding in helping us with our ideas, our terms, and our stories. As you can see in these chapters, this book is all about our friends. In specific we gratefully acknowledge the help of the following people:

John Teter, Tom Hughes, James Choung, Rick Richardson, Geoff Gordon, Greg Campbell, Alex and Susan Van Riesen, Alex Kirk, Al Hsu, Mark Elsdon Dew, Matthew Hemsley, Dora Yiu, Ryan Pfeiffer, Sam Rizk, Kelly Joiner, Eddie Gonzales, Jamie Ladipo, Adam Croft, Greg Johnson, Paul Joyal, Dan McWilliams, Mary Choung, David Suryk, Beth Ann Williams, Wendy Quay, Melodie Marske, Susan Gordon, Kim Porter, Elizabeth Harris, Boston College InterVarsity students 1998–2002, InterVarsity Chapter Growth Alpha and Beta Test campuses and staff, and Bonhomme's whole Alpha crew.

ONLINE SUPPLEMENTAL MATERIALS

Go deeper with *Breaking the Huddle* with resources available online. Visit ivpress.com/breaking-the-huddle for these free bonus materials, activities, and practical exercises.

Notes

INTRODUCTION: A CASE FOR HOPE

[1]C. S. Lewis, *Mere Christianity* (New York: MacMillan, 1952).

[2]Don Everts, *Jesus with Dirty Feet: A Down-to-Earth Look at Christianity for the Curious and Skeptical* (Downers Grove, IL: InterVarsity Press, 1999).

[3]Don Everts and Doug Schaupp, *I Once Was Lost: What Postmodern Skeptics Taught Us About Their Path to Jesus* (Downers Grove, IL: InterVarsity Press, 2008).

[4]See "Evangelism Resources," InterVarsity Christian Fellowship/USA, http://intervarsity.org/page/evangelism-resources.

[5]We recognize that *conversion* is not an adjective (like *huddled* and *witnessing*) and doesn't necessarily roll off the tongue. We also recognize that in some Christian communities the term *conversion* can be problematic. (In such cases, other terms have been used, such as *transformational communities*. We have no problem with people using synonyms that work better in their context.)

CHAPTER 1: HUDDLED COMMUNITIES

[1]Alpha is a relationship-based, process-oriented introduction to Christianity. For more information go to www.alphausa.org.

CHAPTER 4: NURTURE DISCIPLESHIP MOMENTUM

[1]A sincere thank you to Jason Jensen and the InterVarsity Discipleship Steering Committee for their work on this life-changing pattern of growth.

CHAPTER 5: MOBILIZE RELATIONAL EVANGELISM

[1]Melodie Marske, email message, February 12, 2016.

CHAPTER 6: EMBRACE GOD MOVEMENTS

[1]All quotes from Matthew Hemsley taken from a personal interview on July 11, 2015.

[2]A huge thank you to Brian Mann for getting us started on this amazing tool.

[3]Robert Coleman, *The Master Plan of Evangelism* (Grand Rapids: Revell, 2010).

[4]The name *LaFe* comes from the Spanish for "the faith."

CHAPTER 7: ALIGN VISION, STRUCTURES, AND PEOPLE

[1]From a personal interview on August 13, 2015.

[2]BuzzFeedYellow, "People Guess What Christian Phrases Mean," January 30, 2016, www.youtube.com/watch?v=T8gmtrOBcgQ.

CHAPTER 8: LEADING YOUR COMMUNITY THROUGH CHANGE

[1]Chip Heath and Dan Heath, *Switch: How to Change Things When Change Is Hard* (New York: Crown Business, 2010), 27-48.

CHAPTER 9: BE THE CHANGE

[1]Paul D. Stanley and J. Robert Clinton, *Connecting: The Mentoring Relationships You Need to Succeed in Life* (Colorado Springs, CO: NavPress, 1992), 41, 161.

[2]Jim Collins and Morten T. Hansen, *Great by Choice: Uncertainty, Chaos, and Luck—Why Some Thrive Despite Them All* (New York: HarperCollins, 2011).

[3]Tod Bolsinger, *Canoeing the Mountains: Christian Leadership in Uncharted Territory* (Downers Grove, IL: InterVarsity Press, 2015).

[4]Brené Brown, *Rising Strong: The Reckoning. The Rumble. The Revolution* (New York: Spiegel & Grau, 2015), 110-14.

More Titles from InterVarsity Press

I Once Was Lost
978-0-8308-3608-6

Go and Do
978-0-8308-3822-6

Jesus with Dirty Feet
978-0-8308-2206-5

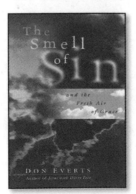

The Smell of Sin
978-0-8308-2389-5

Being White
978-0-8308-3247-7